FRENCH SELF-TAUGHT

By

The Natural Method with Phonetic Pronunciation

THIMM'S SYSTEM

SPECIAL EDITION WITH PHRASES
APPLICABLE TO EMPLOYEES OF
THE CANADIAN PACIFIC RAILWAY

CANADIAN PACIFIC
FOUNDATION LIBRARY EDITION

TORONTO
THE MUSSON BOOK COMPANY LTD.
1937

PREFACE.

THE **aim** of this handbook is to provide all who desire a practical knowledge of the French language with a simple and efficient means of acquiring it, that without having to learn exhaustive vocabularies or complete rules of grammar, they may gain sufficient conversational power to carry them through the common-places of every-day life, and express themselves with confidence both as to the construction of their sentences and the idioms of the language.

The **method** adopted is that which is natural to every child learning to speak his mother-tongue, who long before he learns the rules of grammar acquires one by one a number of words and every-day sentences which enable him to take his part in the talk of the home : so, to meet the requirements of men and women in daily life, vocabularies, phrases, and conversations have been most carefully selected ; and students, instead of learning a vast number of comparatively useless words, will find every word and expression given of such frequent service as to afford facilities of conversation far beyond what might be expected from a book of this size.

The **student** will find at the same time that the phonetic pronunciation, based on scientifically arranged symbols, goes far to remove the difficulties encountered on his first introduction to the language, and greatly facilitates the labours of both teacher and pupil, while to those who cannot avail themselves of the aid of a teacher's voice it will prove an invaluable guide. The English words or sentences, the French equivalents, and the phonetic pronunciation of the French are arranged side by side in three columns, and any difficulty that might arise in reading off the French words correctly at sight, with the aid of the phonetics in the third column, is obviated by means of an explanatory note at the foot of each page.

The book thus also forms a phrase-book altogether suitable to travellers and tourists abroad, who will find, ready to hand and systematically arranged, words and phrases for Travel by road, rail, and sea, for Hotel, Post-Office, Shopping, Amusements, Changing Money, and the many other requirements of

social life: the titles of these classified lists being printed
close to the margins of the right and left-hand pages for the
sake of easy reference when travelling about.

The present edition, while founded upon the celebrated
system of Franz Thimm, has been entirely re-written, re-
vised, and so enlarged, that, although the original section
on grammar has been omitted, the book has been very
considerably increased in size.

The Publishers have had the valuable assistance of
Monsieur J. Laffitte, B.-ès-L., principal French Master at
the City of London School, in reading the proofs.   M.
Laffitte, however, is not responsible for the phonetic pro-
nunciation, the Publishers desiring to retain the now widely
accepted system known as "Marlborough's System of
Phonetics," applied throughout the whole of their SELF-
TAUGHT SERIES of Languages.

In place of the section on Elementary Grammar, which
formed a part of the earlier editions of this book, an entirely
new volume has been prepared, entitled **French Grammar
Self-Taught with a Key to the Exercises*** by M. Laffitte,
and forms a companion volume to the present edition of
French Self-Taught.   The student cannot do better
than work through these books together, thus simultaneous-
ly acquiring a full vocabulary and much conversational
matter, and a practical acquaintance with the rules of
French grammar and the construction of sentences.

In this way the Publishers hope and believe the student
will be enabled to gain a thorough introduction to the
language both as it is spoken and written, which will open
his way to a more extensive study of French literature and
an entire mastery of the French language.

---

* "French Grammer Self-Taught with a Key to the Exercises," by
J. Laffitte, B.-ès-L., Principal French Master, City of London School,
London, E.C.   Uniform with "French Self-Taught."   For home study
and class use.
Cloth $1.50
Toronto; The Musson Book Company Ltd.

CONTENTS

	PAGE
Introductory Remarks, &c.	7
The Phonetic System	7
Pronunciation, Gender, The Articles	8
The Tonic Accent, French Equivalents	9
The Alphabet	9
Vowel Combinations, Diphthongs, etc.	12
Accents and Signs	14
The Nasal Sound	15
Method of Study	16
Vocabularies:	
World and Nature, The	17
Land and Water	18
Minerals and Metals	19
Animals, Birds, Fishes, etc.	20
Reptiles and Insects	22
Fruits, Trees, Flowers, and Vegetables	22
Colours	24
Town and Country	24
Time and Seasons	27
Holidays in France	28
Mankind: Relations	29
Human Body, The	30
Bodily and Mental Powers; Physical Qualities	31
Health	32
Food, Drink, etc.	34
Cooking and Table Utensils	36
Dress and the Toilet	37
Washing List	39
House and Furniture, The	40
Countries and Nations	42
Towns, etc.	43
Travelling by Rail and Road	44
Travelling by Sea	46
Amusements	48
Cycling	50
Motoring	52
Photography	54
Post, Telegraph, and Telephone	56
Correspondence	57
Professions and Trades	58
Commercial Terms	59
Legal Terms	64
Ranks, Titles, etc.	67

CONTENTS

	PAGE
Military Titles	67
Military Terms	68
erms	71
(Cardinal, Ordinal, Collective and Distributive, etc.)	74 to 76
s	76
	82
Conjunctions, and Prepositions	86
of Adjectives, Pronouns, and Auxiliary Verbs	91 to 94

ational Phrases and Sentences:

ngs and Polite Expressions	95
and Necessary Expressions	97
essions of Emotion	101
ing Enquiries	102
e, The	103
Train	104
ssenger Enquiry	105
otel Front Office, In the	114
otel Dining Room, In the	121
arriage Agents	123
Porters and Bell Boys	125
Housekeeper's Department	127
Telegraph Office, In a	128
Ships at Sea	136
Express Office, In an	137
Financial Paper, Expressions in Sale of	149
Ocean Travel	153
Embarking, When	155
On Board Ship	156
Steward	156
Purser	157
Index of Subjects	158

FRENCH SELF-TAUGHT.

Introductory Remarks, etc.

The Phonetic System.—The simplicity of this method of representing the sounds of the French language, will be found to obviate the necessity for spending much time and trouble in mastering and memorising a difficult scheme of phonetics, as a preliminary to understanding from the work itself how to pronounce correctly.

The aim of Marlborough's Phonetic System is to make use of such signs only, that anyone who speaks English will, by reading them naturally, pronounce the French correctly. To prevent confusion arising from the various ways in which sounds are often represented in English, the principle has been laid down that each sound in the new language be separately represented—a principle which may be expressed as *one sound one sign*, and conversely, that each phonetic sign be pronounced in the same manner throughout the book. In any instances where this has been departed from, the reason, usually obvious, is to facilitate ready and correct pronunciation, as in the alternative use of "ah" and "a," "c" and "k," "g" and "gh," "ee" and "y."

The attention of the student may be advantageously drawn to the few arbitrary signs used, viz. the distinguishing of the long "er" sound by marking the e thus, ēr (see page 13), the use of the sign "eū" for the French u (see page 12), and the symbol "n" for the nasal (see page 15). It will be found of great benefit to all to carefully read through the following particulars, which explain the pronunciation of the French and remove any difficulties that might possibly arise as to the exact reading of the phonetic spelling.

To those using the book for temporary purposes only this is not so important, as in the large majority of cases they will already have had some experience of the French language, yet to them also these particulars may prove very useful in readily settling any doubt as to the precise force or sound to be given to any word.

Pronunciation.—The following hints will be useful. **The** phonetics in the third column should be pronounced lightly, not in a laboured manner; thus *ah, ee, oh,* etc., should be light and short, not dwelt upon. Frequent practice in speaking will prove of the greatest assistance, and no opportunity should be lost of perfecting one's accent by hearing the language spoken by an educated native of France.

The NASAL sound so generally used when *n* and *m* occur at the end of a syllable or of a word is of so much importance to every student of French who wishes to acquire a correct pronunciation that a special article has been devoted to it, and will be found on page 15.

Note that the phonetic "a*i*" represents a simple (single) sound, as *a* in *fair, fare,* etc., and that the feminine article *la* is similarly spelt in the phonetics, as "lah," which suggests the right *kind* of sound, is much too *long.*

The sign ⌢ joining two words shows that they must be joined in pronunciation; thus, *des huîtres* (daiz⌢ȇueetr'), *les asperges* (laiz⌢aspairzh).*

The hyphen (-) in the third column is used to facilitate ready and correct pronunciation, and not to show the proper division of the French words into syllables.

The apostrophe (') indicates the suppression of a vowel, or that the consonant to which it is attached is to be distinctly sounded as though followed by a vowel, and must not be confused with the tonic accent.

Gender.—The genders of French nouns are difficult to learn, being masculine and feminine only (there is no neuter as in English); but as the *article* varies in the singular according to the gender of the noun, it has been given attached to the nouns throughout the Vocabularies, and by learning the two together the genders of the nouns will be easily acquired and this obstacle overcome. Where the gender cannot be indicated in this way, " m." for masculine and " f." for feminine has been added to the noun.†

The Articles.—The French Articles are:—Definite, masc. sing. *le* (*l'*), fem. sing. *la* (*l'*), masc. and fem. plural *les*; Indefinite, masc. *un*, fem. *une.*

* This is called the *liaison*—see " French Grammar Self-Taught," pp. 8-9.

† For the plural and feminine of nouns and adjectives see " French Grammar Self-Taught," pp. 16-18 and 20-23 respectively.

The Tonic Accent.—The tonic accent or stress usually falls upon the last syllable in French, but if the last syllable is mute the accent falls on the last but one; this is frequently denoted by the sign (') as in the words *rosée* (rohzeh'), *ténèbres* (teh-nai'br').

French Equivalents.—It should be noted that many of the French phrases in the latter part of the book are not literal translations of the English, but the French equivalents, i.e. what a Frenchman would say in similar circumstances.

The Alphabet.

The French Alphabet consists of 25 letters :—

Characters.	Name and English Pronunciation.	Phonetics used.
A, a	(ah) When long like *a* in *father*; as *casser* (cahsseh), *parer* (pah'reh)	ah, a
	When short like *a* in *man*; as *chapeau* (shap-oh)...	a
B, b	(ber*) as in English	b
C, c	(ser) like *k* before *a, o, u,* or a consonant; as *canard* (can-ahrr), *côte* (coht), *écrire* (eh-creer)...	c, k
	Before *e, i* and *y*, and when written with a cedilla (*ç*), like *s* in *sun, mist*; as *cerize* (ser-reez), *façade* (fassahd), *cygne* (seenyer)	s, ss
	(See also *ch*, p. 13.)	
D, d	(der) mostly as in English	d
	Final *d*, when joined to a following word commencing with a vowel or *h* mute, is pronounced like *t*; otherwise it is silent: e.g., *grand* (grahn), *grand homme* (grahn-tum)	t
E, e	(ai) has (1) an open sound before *r*, like *a* in *fair*, as *merci* (mairsee), *hiver* (eevair) ; in *et* final, as *buffet* (beüffai) ; and in *des, les, mes, ces,* etc. (da*i*, la*i*, ma*i*, sa*i*)	†ai

---

* The modern names of the French letters are phonetic; those of the consonants are respectively pronounced like *be, ce, de, fe,* in tu*b*er, ni*c*er, ri*d*er, wa*f*er, etc.

† "*r*" and "*i*" in italic type (*r, i*) are not to be sounded at all; "*y*" is added to "*a*" and "*i*" to "*a*" to give those letters the sounds desired, viz., of "e" in *father* and "a" in *air* respectively.

Characters.	Name and English Pronunciation.	Phonetics used.

(2) a short, sharp sound like *e* in *bell*; as *ciel* (s'yell), *lettre* (lettr') ... ...   **e**

In *de*, *le*, *je*, *me*, and the prefix *re*, etc., it is like the *e* in *brother*; thus—der, ler, zher, mer, rer ...   ***er**

In the final *er* of verbs, *e* has a close sound, the *r* being silent, as *couper* (coopeh), *aller* (alleh)   **eh**

Final *e* in a word or syllable is silent, but in many cases it vocalizes the preceding consonant, which otherwise would not be sounded; thus *achetez* (ash-teh); and compare *lent* (lahn) and *lente* (lahnt), *petit* (p'tee) and *petite* (p'teet).

É, é, is pronounced "eh," like *a* in *Sunday* spoken with the *teeth nearly closed*; e.g., thé (teh), *été* (eh-teh) ... ...   **eh**

È, è, is like the first *e* in *there*; as in *père* (pair)...⎫
Ê, ê, is like the simple (long and open) sound of *a* ⎬ ***ai**
in *bale*; as *tête* (tait) ... ... ⎭

F, f —(fer) as in English; sounded when final ...   **f**

G, g—(zher) hard before *a*, *o*, *u*, or a consonant; as *goût* (goo), *grêle* (grail) ... ... **g, gh**

Soft like *s* in *pleasure*, before *e*, *i* and *y*; as *neige* (naizh), *agile* (azh-eel) ... ...   **zh**

Silent *e* is sometimes retained after *g* when followed by another vowel, in order to preserve the soft sound of the *g*, as in *mangeons* (mahn-zhon).

H, h—(her) is practically unaspirated in actual speech†; and *th* is pronounced as *t*, e.g. *méthode* (meh-tod).

I, i —(ee) is usually like *ee* in *meet*; as *mille* (meel)...   **ee**

In *iens* in verbs, *ierre*, *ier* and *iers* in words of one syllable, it is like the *i* in *junior*, having the effect of *y*, as *chien* (sh'yan), *pierre* (p'yair) ...   **y**

J, j — (zher) like *s* in *vision*; as *bijou* (bee-zhoo) ...   **zh**

K, k—(ker) as in English ... ...   **k**

L, l —(ler) usually as in English; as *lait* (lai), *ville* (veel)   **l**

Sometimes, and especially when double and preceded by *i*, it has the effect in the middle of a word of the *i* in *junior* (i.e., like *y*); as *ailleurs* (ah-yĕrr)   **y**

Characters.	Name and English Pronunciation.	Phonetics used.

When final and preceded by *i* it is like *ee*, as *soleil* (so-lai'ee or so-lay'), *travail* (trahvah'ee) ... **ee, y**

M, m—(me*r*) as in English, except in the nasal syllables *am, aim, em, im, om, um*, for which see p. 14 ... **m**

N, n—(ne*r*) as in English, except in nasal syllables ... **n**

O, o—(oh) when short like *u* in *dull*; as *pomme* (pum) **u**

When long like *o* in *polo*; as *opéra* (oh-peh-rah) ... **oh**

P, p—(pe*r*) as English. (See *ph*, p. 14) ... ... **p**

Q, q—(ke*r*) as in English. Initially it is always followed by *u*, which as a rule is silent; e.g. *querelle* (kerell') **k**

R, r—(re*r*) as in English, but MORE STRONGLY ARTICULATED ... ... **r, rr**

It is usually silent in the termination *er*, except when followed by a word beginning with a vowel or *h* mute; e.g., *premier* = prerm-yeh, but *premier ordre* = prerm-yair ordr'.

S, s—(se*r*) is always like *s* in *sister*, except between two vowels or when used to make liaison with a word following, when it is like *z*. Examples: *sept* (set), *ouest* (oo-est), *cristal* (cristahl); *brosse* (bross) ... ... **s, ss**

Exceptions: *rose* (rohz), *raison* (raizon), *vous avez* (voo-zav-eh), *mes amis* (mai zam-ee) ... ... **z**

Final *s* is usually silent, unless used to make liaison with a word following: e.g. *bas* (bah), *fleuves* (flerv), *commis* (commee); compare *les* (lai) and *les arbres* (lai zahrbr'). In a few words final *s* is sounded even when they stand alone, and in these instances the *s* is as in *sister*; e.g. *ours* (oorss), *Reims* (ranss).

T, t—(te*r*) usually as in English ... ... **t**

In some words where in English *t* sounds like *sh*, in French it is a simple sibilant; e.g., *nation* (nah-s'yon) ... ... **s'**

After *s* and in certain tenses of verbs it remains hard; as *question* (kess-t'yon) *partions* (pahrr-t'yon) ... ... **t**

Final *t* is silent except before a vowel sound, and even then it is not sounded if preceded by *r*; as *faut* (foh), *faut-il* (foh-teel), *tort* (tohr), *à tort et à travers* (ah tohr ai ah travair).

Characters.	Name and English Pronunciation.	Phonetics used.

U, u — (eũ) There is no sound in English exactly corresponding with the French *u*. It is something like the Scotch *u* in *gude*. To produce it, form the lips as for whistling and pronounce *eu* (or *ew*) as one sound   ...   .   **eũ**

In words like *cuisine*, *u* has the same sound but **very light**; it is *not* the sound of *w* (i.e, ŏŏ short).

In the nasal syllables *un, um*, it is like *u* in *fur* ...   **u**

V, v — (ver) usually as in English   ...   .   **v**

X, x — (kser) usually as in English; as *taxer* (taxeh) ...   **x**

In *deux* (dēr), *dix* (deess), *six* (seess), and other adjectives, when followed by a word beginning with a vowel sound, it is pronounced like *z*; e.g., *beaux* (boh), *beaux yeux* (boh-zee-ēr'), *dix-huit* (dee-zeũeet)   ...   .   **z**

Silent before a consonant; e.g., *dix sous* (dee soo).

Y, y — (yer), standing alone, or at the beginning of a word, or after a consonant, is like *ee* in *meet* (short); as *y* (ee), *yeux* (ee-ēr'), *style* (steel)   ...   **ee**

After a vowel it has a strong *y* sound almost like *y-y* in *pay you*; as *rayon* (raiyon)   ...   ...   **y**

Z, z — (zer) as in English   ...   .   **z**

Final *z* is usually silent unless followed by a word beginning with a vowel sound and employed to make liaison; as *avez* (av-eh), *avez eu* (av-eh-zeũ).

Vowel Combinations, Diphthongs, etc.

VOWEL COMBINATIONS.—The following each represent one sound :—

Combination.	Pronunciation.	Phonetics used.

ai, ei ... are like *a* in *aim*; e.g., *lait* (lai), *Seine* (sain)...   **ai**

Except in nasal syllables, which see; for *ail* and *eil* see above under L, l.

ai has also the sound of *é* (p. 9), e.g. *j'ai* (zheh).

au, eau, are pronounced *oh*; as *taureau* (tohroh), *épaule* (eh-pohl), *couteau* (koo-toh)   ...   .   **oh**

NOTE.—The French have not the sound of *aw* or *au* in *raw, taught, hall*, etc. Thus *Paul* is pronounced "pohl," *auteur* is "oh-tērr."

Combination.	Pronunciation.	Phonetics used.

eu, œu, resemble *u* in *turn* or *e* in *herd*; as in *peu*
(pēr), *cœur* (kērr), except *eu*, had (= ēū)   ...   *ēr

ou   ... is like *oo* in *boot*; as *nouveau* (noo-voh),
souris (soo-ree)   ...   .   oo

DIPHTHONGS.—The following table shows the sounds of
which each diphthong is composed:—

Diphthong.   French sounds.

ia   =   *i* + *a* (short ee + ah), as in *viande* (vee-ahnd).

iai   =   *i* + *è* (ee + a*i*), as *liaison* (lee-ai-zon).

ié   =   *i* + *é* (ee + eh SHORT AND CLOSED), as *prié*
                 (pree'eh).

iè   =   *i* + *è* (ee + a*i*), as *pièce* (pee-aiss).

Similarly, in each of the following the division occurs after
the *i*, each diphthong representing two sounds—in some cases
the nasal being added also:

io—e.g., *idiot* (eed-ee-oh).   ien—e.g., *bien* (bee-an').

ian—*expédiant* (ex-ped-ee-   ient—*patient* (pah-see-ahn).
        ahn).   ieu—*lieu* (lee-er').

iau—*miauler* (mee-oh-leh).   ion—*portion* (pohr-see-on).

oi   =   *o* + *a* (oh, *almost silent,* + ah).

Preceded by a consonant *oi* sounds very like *wah*; as
foi [f(oh)-ah or fwah].

oin   =   *o* + *in* (oh, *almost silent,* + an); as *loin* (lwan).

oua   =   *ou* + *a* (oo + ah); as *secoua* (ser-koo-ah).

oui   =   *ou* + *i* (oo + ee); as *Louis* (loo-ee).

ua   =   *u* + *a* (ēū + ah); as *nuage* (nēū-ahzh).

ui   =   *u* + *i* (ēū + ee); as *pluie* (plēū-ee).

uin   =   *u* + *in* (ēū + an); as *Juin* (zhēū-an).

* See footnote on silent *s* and *t*, p. 8.

COMBINATIONS OF CONSONANTS.—These are as follows:—

Combination.	Pronunciation.	Phonetics used.
ch — usually like *sh* ; as *bouche* (boosh), *chaque* (shahk)		sh
gn — almost like *ny* in *Bunyan* ; as *agneau* (ahnyoh)		ny
ll — after *i*, like *ee* short or *y*; as *tailleur* (tah-yĕrr) ...		ee, y
ph — like *f*; as *phare* (fahr)		f

Accents and Signs.

ACCENTS.—The French language has three accents, which are used with *a, e, i, o,* and *u,* either to modify their pronunciation or for the purpose of distinguishing between words spelt alike, but having different meanings. They are :

1. The **Acute** accent (´), used only on *e,* to give it a *close* sound, i.e., as if spoken with the teeth nearly closed ; as *épée* (eh-peh´). The acute accent often has the effect of giving a more or less sharp and distinct sound to *e* when it would otherwise be either silent or almost unheard. Compare *café* and *cape, ouvré* and *ouvre, donné* and *donne, aisément* and *lentement.*

2. The **Grave** accent (`), used on *e* to give it an *open* sound, as *père* (pair) ; and on *a* and *u* to distinguish between words otherwise spelt alike. Compare *la* (lah), the, and *là* (lah), there ; *ou* (oo), or, and *où* (oo), where.

3. The **Circumflex** accent (^), used on any vowel except *y* to give it a *long, open* sound; as in *âge* (ahzh), *tête* (tait), *maître* (maitr´), *impôt* (anpoh), *flûte* (fleut).

The French *e* without an accent at the end of a word or syllable is often silent ; *with* an accent it is always sounded, as explained above.

SIGNS.—The **Cedilla** (˛) is a sign placed under *c*—thus *ç*—when followed by *a, o,* or *u,* to indicate that it must be pronounced soft or like *s* ; as *garçon* (gahr-son), *façade* (fassahd), *reçu* (rer-sēu).

The **Apostrophe** (´) is a sign showing the suppression of a vowel where necessary for the sake of euphony ; thus, *l'ami* (lah-mee) instead of *le ami.*

The **Diaeresis** (¨), placed over the second of two vowels following each other, indicates that they are to be pronounced separately. Compare *naïf* (nah-eef) with *lait* (lai).

The Nasal Sound.

There being no sound in English exactly resembling the French nasal, it is impossible to represent it accurately by means of our letters. It is something between the sound made in the nose when we clearly pronounce the *n* in *no, ran, gone, find*, and the sound of *ng* in *sang, song, sung*. By speaking these last three words as much as possible *through the nose*, and cutting off the guttural *g*, we get pretty near the correct sound.

The nasal is represented in French both by *n* and *m*, but nasal *m* is pronounced exactly like nasal *n*. By attaching this nasal to the vowels *a* (or *e*), *i, o, u*, we get four nasal *combinations* or *syllables*—sometimes spoken of as the "nasal sounds" —viz., *an* (or *en*), *in, on, un*, which are the sounds in *sahng, sang, song*, and *sung*, pronounced as described above. (The *u* in "sung" should be slightly dwelt on, almost as if spelt "surng.")

There are many combinations in French which contain the nasal sound, but they are all pronounced like one or other of the four just given, which may therefore be regarded as the types. Thus:

Like **an**...*en, am, em, ean, aen* and *aon*, the phonetic for which is ... ... ahn
„ **in** ...*im, ain, aim, ein, ym*, and sometimes *en** ... an
„ **on**...*om, eon* (after *g*, the *e* being silent) ... ... on
„ **un**...*um, eun* ... ... un

Thus, throughout this book every nasal combination is represented in the third or pronunciation column by one of the phonetic signs : ahn, an, on, un.

The following words exemplify the various forms of the nasal :—

1. Words containing the sound of *an* (ahn)

langue (lahng')	*diamant* (d'yah-mahn)
manteau (mahntoh)	*gants* (gahn)
enfant (ahn-fahn)	*chambre* (shahnbr')
ambulance (ahnbeulahnss)	*dent* (dahn)
sentir (sahnteer)	*temps* (tahn)
embarquer (ahnbahrkeh)	*Jean* (zhahn)
mangeant (mahn-zhahn)	*Caen* (kahn)
faon (fahn)	*faisan* (faizahn)

* I.e., in words terminating in *en* or *ien*, and in the verbs *tenir* and *venir* and their compounds as *tiens* (tee-an), *viens* (vee-an).

2. Words having the sound of *in* (an).

singe (sanzh)
moulin (moolan)
loin (lwan)
imprimer (anpreemeh)
maintenant (mant'nahn)
frein (fran)
mien (mee-an)

incendie (ansahndee)
moins (mwan)
timbre (tanbr')
pain (pan)
faim (fan)
symbole (san-bol)
tiens (tee-an)

3. Words with the sound of *on* (on).

monde (mond)
pigeon (pee-zhon)
ombrage (onbrahzh)

lion (lee-on)
onzième (on-zee-aim)
concombre (konkonb

4. Words containing the sound of *un* (un).

un, the masculine article
(un, before words begin-
ning with consonant only)

lundi (lundee)
alun (al-un)

NOTE.—When *n* (or *m*) is followed by another *n* or *m*, or by a vowel, it is NOT NASAL; e.g.,

inactif (een-ak-teef)
bonne (bun)
imiter (eemeeteh)
pomme (pum)

innocent (een-oh-sahn)
donner (donneh)
immédiat (eem-meh-d'yah)
monument (moh-neū-mahn)

Method of Study.—The student is recommended to learn the words in the following Vocabularies by heart, repeating them *aloud* with the aid of the phonetic spelling in the third column, and then closing the book, write out the French words with their proper spelling from memory, carefully comparing with and correcting by the French column afterwards. In this way a very large number of French words will be acquired, the ear being familiarized with their sound, the tongue with their utterance, and the eye with their appearance. The same plan can then be followed with the Conversational Phrases and Sentences, and imaginary conversations worked out by the substitution of other nouns, adjectives, adverbs, etc., which have already been learned from the Vocabularies.

VOCABULARIES.*

The World and Nature
Le monde et la Nature

English.	French.	Pronunciation.
The air	l'air m.	lair
the climate	le climat	ler cleemah
the cloud	le nuage	ler neŭahzh
the cold	le froid	ler frwah
the darkness	les ténèbres f.pl.	lai teh-naïbr'
the dew	la rosée	la roh-zeh'
the earth	la terre	la taïr
the east	l'est m.	laïst
an eclipse	une éclipse	ēun eh-cleeps
the fire	le feu	ler fēr
the fog	le brouillard	ler broo-yar
the frost	la gelée	la zh'leh'
the hail	la grêle	la graïl
the heat	la chaleur	la shal-ērr
the ice	la glace	la glahss
the light	la lumière	la lēum-yaïr
the lightning	l'éclair m.	leh-claïr
the moon	la lune	la lēun
the moonlight	le clair de lune	ler clair-der-lēun
the north	le nord	ler nor
the rain	la pluie	la plēuee'
the rainbow	l'arc-en-ciel m.	lar-kahn-s'yel
the shade	l'ombrage m.	lon-brahzh
a shadow	une ombre	ēun onbr'
the sky	le ciel	ler s'yel
the snow	la neige	la naïzh
the south	le sud	ler sēud
a star	une étoile	ēun eh-twahl
the sun	le soleil	ler soh-lay (soh-leh-ee)
a thaw	un dégel	un deh-zhel
the thunder	le tonnerre	ler tonnaïr
the west	l'ouest m.	lwaïst
the wind	le vent	ler vahn

* The gender of the nouns is in most cases shown by the Article attached.

Italic r and i silent; thick n indicates nasal; apostrophe indicates suppressed vowel.

Land and Water   La terre et l'eau

English.	French.	Pronunciation.
The bank (of river)	la rive	la reev
a bay	une baie	eūn bai
the beach	la plage	la plahzh
a calm	un calme	un cal-m'
the canal	le canal	ler can-al
a cape, headland	un cap	un cap
the cliff	la falaise	la fal-aiz
the coast	la côte	la coht
the current	le courant	ler coorahn
the ebb	le reflux	ler rerfleū
the flow (rising tide)	le flux	ler fleū
a hill	une colline	eūn colleen
an island	une île	eūn eel
the lake	le lac	ler lak
the mainland	le continent	ler con-tee-nahn
a marsh	un marais	un marai
a mountain	une montagne	eūn mon-tahn-yer
the ocean	l'océan m.	loh-seh-ahn
a peninsula	une presqu'île	eūn press-keel
the river	le fleuve	ler flērv
a rock	un roc	un rok
the sand	le sable	ler sab-l'
a sand-bank	un banc de sable	un bahnc d' sab-l'
the sea	la mer	la mair
the sea-shore	les bords de la mer	lai bohrd'lam-air
the shingle	le galet	ler gal-ai
the shore	le rivage	ler ree-vahzh
a storm	une tempête [seau	eūn tahnpait [soh'
the stream	la rivière, le ruis-	la reevyair, ler reūee-
the thunderstorm	l'orage m.	loh-rahzh
the tide	la marée	la marreh'
high tide	haute marée	oht marreh'
low tide	basse marée	bass marreh'
a valley	une vallée	eūn valleh'
the water	l'eau f.	loh
fresh water	l'eau douce	loh dooss
salt water	l'eau salée	loh sal-eh'
a waterfall	une cascade	eūn cascahd
the wave	la vague	la vahg

Minéraux et métaux — Minerals and Metals

English.	French.	Pronunciation.
The aluminium	l'aluminium m.	laleūmeen-yun
the brass	l'airain m.	lairan
the bronze	le bronze	ler bronz
the chalk	la craie	la crai
the clay	l'argile f.	lar-zheel
the coal	le charbon	ler shar-bon
the copper	le cuivre	ler kēueevr'
the coral	le corail	ler coh-rah-ee
the crystal	le cristal	ler criss-tal
the glass	le verre	ler vair
the gold	l'or m.	lor
the granite	le granit	ler graneet
the gravel	le gravier	ler grav-yai
the iron	le fer	ler fair
cast iron	la fonte	la font
wrought iron	le fer forgé	ler fair for-zheh
the lead	le plomb	ler plon
the lime	la chaux	la shoh
the marble	le marbre	ler mar-br'
mercury, quicksil-	le mercure, vif-ar-	ler mair-kēur, veef-ar-
the nickel　[ver	le nickel　[gent	ler nee-kel　[zhahn
the silver	l'argent m.	lar-zhahn
the silver-plate	l'argenterie f.	larzhahnt'ree
the slate	l'ardoise f.	lardwahz
the soda	la soude	la sood
the steel	l'acier m.	lass'yeh
the stone	la pierre	la p'yair
stones, precious	pierres précieuses	p'yair preh-s'yērz
the amethyst	l'améthyste f.	lam-eh-teest
the carbuncle	l'escarboucle f.	lesscarboocl'
the diamond	le diamant	ler d'yam-ahn
the emerald	l'émeraude f.	lehm'rohd
an opal	une opale	ēun oh-pal
the pearl	la perle	la pairl
a ruby	un rubis	un rēubee
the sapphire	le saphir	ler saf-eer
the turquoise	la turquoise	la tēurkwahz
the tin	l'étain m.	leh-tan
the zinc	le zinc	ler zank

Italic *r* and *i* silent; thick **n** indicates nasal; apostrophe indicates suppressed vowel.　　C*

Animals, Birds, Fishes, &c. Animaux, oiseaux, poissons, &c.

(For *Dining* see p. 111.)

English.	French.	Pronunciation.
A bear	*un ours*	ern oorss
a blackbird	*un merle*	un mairl
a bull	*un taureau*	un toh-roh
a calf	*un veau*	un voh
the cat	*le chat*	ler shah
a chicken	*un poulet*	un poo-lai
the claw	*la griffe*	la greef
a cock	*un coq*	un cok
a cod	*une morue*	eūn moreū
a cow	*une vache*	eūn vash
a crab	*une écrevisse*	eūn eh-crer-veess
the cries	*les cris* m.	lai cree
the barking	*l'aboiement* m.	lab-wah-mahn
the bleating	*le bêlement*	ler bailmahn
the braying	*le braiment*	ler brai-mahn
the crowing [ing	*le chant du coq*	ler shahn deū cok
growling, grunt-	*grognement* m.	gron-y'mahn
the howling	*le hurlement*	ler heūrl'mahn
the mewing	*le miaulement*	ler mee-ohl-mahn
the neighing	*le hennissement*	ler hanneessmahn
a cuckoo	*un coucou*	un coo-coo
a deer	*un daim*	un dan
the dog	*le chien*	ler sh'yan
a donkey	*un âne*	ern ahn
the dove	*la colombe*	la col-onb
a duck	*un canard*	un can-arr
the eagle	*l'aigle* m.	lai-gl'
an eel	*une anguille*	eūn ahn-ghee-y'
an elephant	*un éléphant*	ern eh-leh-fahn
a feather	*une plume*	eūn pleūm
the fox	*le renard*	ler ren-arr
a goat	*une chèvre*	eūn shaivr'
a goose	*une oie*	eūn wah
a grouse	*un coq de bruyère*	un cok d' breū-yair
a gull	*une mouette*	eūn moo-et
a haddock	*une merluche*	eūn mair-leūsh
the hare	*le lièvre*	ler lee-aivr'
a hen	*une poule*	eūn pool

English.	French.	Pronunciation.
a herring	*un hareng*	un harrahn
the hoof	*le sabot*	ler sahboh
the horn	*la corne*	la cohrn
a horse	*un cheval*	un sh'val
a lamb	*un agneau*	ern an-yoh
a lark	*une alouette*	eūn al-oo-et'
a lion	*un lion*	un lee-on
a lobster	*un homard*	un oh-mar
the mane	*la crinière*	la creen-yair
a monkey	*un singe*	un sanzh
the mouse	*la souris*	la soo-ree
a nightingale	*un rossignol*	un rosseenyol
an owl	*un hibou*	un heeboo
an ox	*un bœuf*	un berf
oysters	*des huîtres* f.	daiz eūeetr'
the parrot	*le perroquet*	ler pairrokai
a partridge	*une perdrix*	eūn pair-dree
the paw	*la patte*	la pat
a peacock	*un paon*	un pahn
the pheasant	*le faisan*	ler faizahn
a pig	*un cochon*	un coshon
a pigeon	*un pigeon*	un pee-zhon
a pike	*un brochet*	un broshai
a rabbit	*un lapin*	un lap-an
the rat	*le rat*	ler rah
a rook	*une corneille*	eūn cor-nai-ee-y'
a salmon	*un saumon*	un sohmon
salt fish	*du poisson salé*	deū pwah-son sal-eh
a sheep	*un mouton*	un moo-ton
the shell-fish	*le crustacé*	ler creūstasseh'
the snipe	*la bécassine*	la bec-asseen'
a sole	*une sole*	eūn sol
the sparrow	*le moineau*	ler mwah-noh
the swallow	*l'hirondelle* f.	leerondel'
a swan	*un cygne*	un seen-y'
the tail	*la queue*	la kēr
a thrush	*une grive*	eūn greev
a tiger	*un tigre*	un teegr'
a trout	*une truite*	eūn treūeet
a turbot	*un turbot*	un teūrboh
a turkey	*un dindon*	un dan-don

Italic *r* and *s* silent; thick n indicates nasal; apostrophe indicates suppressed vowel.

English.	French.	Pronunciation.
a turtle, tortoise	*une tortue*	ēūn tohr-tēū
a whale	*une baleine*	ēūn bal-ain
a whiting	*un merlan*	un mairlahn
a wing	*une aile*	ēūn ail
a wolf	*un loup*	un loo

Reptiles & Insects　　Reptiles et insectes

An ant	*une fourmi*	ēūn foor-mee
a bee	*une abeille*	ēūn ab-ai-ee-y'
a beetle	*un scarabée*	un scar-ah-beh'
a butterfly	*un papillon*	un pap-ee-yon
a caterpillar	*une chenille*	ēūn sh'nee-y'
a flea	*une puce*	ēūn pēūss
a fly	*une mouche*	ēūn moosh
a frog	*une grenouille*	ēūn grer-noo-ee'y'
a gnat	*un moucheron*	un moo-sh'ron
the grasshopper	*la sauterelle*	la soht'rell
an insect	*un insecte*	ern ansect
a mosquito	*un moustique*	un moosteek
a moth	*une mite*	ēūn meet
a silkworm	*un ver à soie*	un vair ah swah
a snail	*un limaçon*	un leemass'on
a snake	*une couleuvre*	ēūn coo-lērvr'
a spider	*une araignée*	ēūn arrain-yeh'
the sting	*l'aiguillon* m.	laigēūee-yon
the toad	*le crapaud*	ler crap-oh
a wasp	*une guêpe*	ēūn gaip
a worm	*un ver*	un vair

Fruits, Trees, Flowers & Vegetables
Fruits, arbres, fleurs et légumes　(For "Shopping" see page 119; Meals, pp. 110—116.)

An almond	*une amande*	ēūn am-ahnd
an apple	*une pomme*	ēūn pum
an apricot	*un abricot*	ern ab-ree-coh
an ash	*un frêne*	un frain
the asparagus	*les asperges* f.pl.	laiz aspairzh
the beans	*les fèves* f.pl.	lai faiv
the beech	*le hêtre*	ler haitr'
the beetroot	*les betteraves* f.pl.	lai bett'rav
the birch	*le bouleau*	ler booloh
a blackberry	*une mûre*	ēūn mēūr

Italic *r* and *t* silent; thick n indicates nasal; apostrophe indicates suppressed vowel.

English.	French.	Pronunciation.
a bouquet	*un bouquet*	un boo-kai
a branch	*une branche*	eun brahnsh
a bunch, cluster	*une grappe*	eun grapp
a buttercup	*un bouton d'or*	un booton dor
the cabbage	*le chou*	ler shoo
a carrot	*une carotte*	eun carot'
the cauliflower	*le chou-fleur*	ler shoo-flerr
the celery	*le céleri*	ler sel'ree
a cherry	*une cerise*	eun ser-reez
a chestnut	*une châtaigne*	eun shah-tain-y'
a chestnut-tree	*un châtaignier*	un shatainyeh
the cucumber	*le concombre*	ler con-con-br'
the currant	*la groseille*	la grozai-ee-y'
a daisy	*une marguerite*	eun mar-g'reet
the elm	*l'orme* m.	lorm
an evergreen (shrub)	*un arbuste toujours vert*	ern ar-beust too-zhoor vair
a fern	*une fougère*	eun foo-zhair
a fig	*une figue*	eun feeg
a fruit-tree	*un arbre fruitier*	ern ar-br' freueet-yeh
a gooseberry	*une groseille à maquereau*	eun grozai-ee-y' ah mahkroh
a grape	*un raisin*	un raizan
the holly	*le houx*	ler hoo
the ivy	*le lierre*	ler l-yair
a leaf	*une feuille*	eun fer-ee'y'
a lemon	*un citron*	un seetron
the lettuce	*la laitue*	la laiteu
a lily	*un lis*	un leess
lily-of-the-valley	*le muguet*	ler meu-gai
a melon	*un melon*	un m'lon
a mulberry	*une mûre*	eun meur
a nut, walnut	*une noix*	eun nwah
the oak	*le chêne*	ler shain
an onion	*un oignon*	ern un-yon
an orange	*une orange*	eun ohrahnzh
a parsnip	*un panais*	un pan-ai
a peach	*une pêche*	eun paish
a pear	*une poire*	eun pwahr
the peas	*les pois* m.pl.	lai pwah
a pine	*un pin*	un pan

Italic *r* and *i* silent; thick *n* indicates nasal; apostrophe indicates suppressed vowel.

English.	French.	Pronunciation.
the pine-apple	*l'ananas* m.	lan-an-ah
a plant	*une plante*	eūn plahnt
a plum	*une prune*	eūn preūn
the potato	*la pomme de terre*	la pum der ta*i*r
the radishes	*les radis* m.pl.	la*i* rad-ee
a raspberry	*une framboise*	eūn frahn-bwahz
the root	*la racine*	la rasseen
a rose	*une rose*	eūn roz
the spinach	*les épinards* m.pl.	la*i*z‿eh-pee-**nar**
the stalk, stem	*la tige*	la teezh
a strawberry	*une fraise*	eūn fra*i*z
a tree-trunk	*un tronc*	un tronk
a tulip	*une tulipe*	eūn teūleep
a turnip	*un navet*	un nav-a*i*
the vine	*la vigne*	la veen-y'
a violet	*une violette*	eūn vee-ol-et'

Colours   Les couleurs

Black	*noir* m., *-e* f.	nwahr
blue	*bleu, -e*	blēr
brown	*brun, -e*	brun, breūn
crimson	*cramoisi, -e*	kram-wah-zee'
dark	*foncé, -e*	fon'seh
fawn	*fauve*	fohv
green	*vert, -e*	vair, va*i*rt
grey	*gris, -e*	gree, greez
light	*clair, -e*	clair
orange	*orange*	ohrahnzh
pink	*rose*	roz
purple	*pourpre*	poor'pr°
red	*rouge*	roozh
scarlet	*écarlate*	eh-car-lat'
violet	*violet, -te*	vee'ol-a*i*, vee-ol-ett'
white	*blanc, -he*	blahn, blahnsh
yellow	*jaune*	zhohn

Town and Country   La ville et la campagne   (See "In Town," p. 115.)

The bank (money)	*la banque*	la bahnk
a bank (earth)	*un talus*	un tal-eū
the barley	*l'orge* f.	lohrzh
the barn	*la grange*	la grahnzh

English.	French.	Pronunciation.
the bridge	le pont	ler pon
the building	le bâtiment	ler bahteemahn
the bush	le buisson	ler bẽuee'son
a castle	un château	un shahtoh'
the cattle [tion	le bétail	ler beh-tah'ee
the club; associa-	le club ; le cercle	ler clẽub; ler saircl'
the corn	le blé	ler bleh
a cottage	une chaumière	ẽun shohmee-air
the country	la campagne	la cahn-pahn'y'
the courtyard	la cour	la coor
a crop	une récolte	ẽun rehcolt'
the dining-rooms	le restaurant	ler restorahn
a ditch	un fossé	un fosseh
the dust	la poussière	la pooss-yair
a factory	une manufacture	ẽun mahnẽu-fac'tẽur
a farm	une ferme	ẽun fairm
a farmer	un fermier	un fairmee-eh
a fence	une barrière	ẽun barreeair
the field	le champ	ler shahn
the fisherman	le pêcheur	ler paishẽrr
a flock, herd	un troupeau	un troopoh
the foot-pavement	le trottoir	ler trot-wahr
the forest	la forêt	la forai
the garden	le jardin	ler zhar'dan
the gate	la barrière	la barreeair
the grass	l'herbe f.	lairb
the harvest	la moisson	la mwah'son
hay	le foin	ler fwan
a hedge	une haie	ẽun ai
the high-road	le grand-chemin	ler grahn-sh'man
the hut	la cabane	la cab-ahn'
the inn	l'auberge f.	loh-bairzh
a labourer	un homme de peine	ern um d' pain
a lamp (street-)	un réverbère	un reh-vairbair'
the land	la terre	la tair
the log	la bûche	la bẽush
the manure	le fumier	ler fẽumee-eh
the market	le marché	ler mar'sheh
the market-place	la place du marché	la plahss dẽu mar'sheh
the meadow	le pré	ler preh
the mill	le moulin	ler moolan

Italic *v* and *t* silent; thick n indicates nasal; apostrophe indicates suppressed vowel.

English.	French.	Pronunciation.
a monument	*un monument*	un mo-neū-mahn
the mud	*la boue, vase*	la boo, vaz
the oats	*l'avoine* f.	lav-wahn
an omnibus	*un omnibus*	ern͡ omnee-beūs
the palace	*le palais*	ler pal'a*i*
the park	*le parc*	ler park
a path (footpath)	*un sentier*	un sahnt'yeh
peasant	*paysan* m., *-ne* f.	payeezahn, payeezan'
the pier	*la jetée*	la͡ zh'teh
a place, spot	*un endroit*	ern͡ ahndrwah
a plough	*une charrue*	eūn sharreū'
the police-station	*le poste* (*de police*)	ler posst (der poleess)
the prison	*la prison*	la preezon
the public-house	*le cabaret*	ler cab-ar-a*i*
the railway	*le chemin de fer*	ler sh'man d' fa*i*r
the river	*la rivière*	la reevyair
the road	*la route*	la root
the rye	*le seigle*	ler sai'gl'
the school	*l'école* f.	leh'col
the seed	*la graine*	la grain
the shepherd	*le berger*	ler bair-zheh
a shop	*une boutique*	eūn booteek'
the soil	*la terre*	la tair
a square	*une place*	eūn plahss
a stable (horses')	*une écurie*	eūn eh-keū-ree
livery-stable	*écurie de chevaux de louage; remise*	eh-keū-ree der sh'voh d' lwahzh; rermeez
the straw	*la paille*	la pah'ee-y'
the street	*la rue*	la reū
the timber	*le bois*	ler bwah
the tower	*la tour*	la toor
the town-hall	*l'hôtel de ville*	loh-tel der veel
a tram (car)	*un tram*	un tram
the university	*l'université* f.	leūneevair'seeteh
the village	*le village*	ler vee'lahzh
a vineyard	*un vignoble*	un veenyoh'bl'
a wall	*un mur*	un meūr
a well	*un puits*	un peūee
the wheat	*le (blé-) froment*	ler (bleh-) from-ahn
a windmill	*un moulin à vent*	un moolan ah vahn
the wood	*le bois*	ler bwah

Le temps et les saisons — Time and Seasons

(For Conversations see pp. 137—141.)

English.	French.	Pronunciation.
The afternoon	l'après-midi m.	lap'rai- mee'dee
the birthday	l'anniversaire (de naissance)	lannee-vair-sair (der naissahnss)
Christmas Eve	la veille de Noël	la vai-ee-y' der noh-el'
dawn	l'aurore f.	loh-rorr
the day [row	le jour	ler zhoor
day after to-mor-	après-demain	ap'rai-d'man
the day before yesterday	l'avant-hier	lavahntyair
days of the week	jours de la semaine	zhoor der la s'main
Sunday	dimanche	deemahn'sh
Monday	lundi	lun'dee
Tuesday	mardi	mar'dee
Wednesday	mercredi	mair'crerdee
Thursday	jeudi	zhērdee
Friday	vendredi	vahndrerdee
Saturday	samedi	sahmdee
Easter	Pâques m.	pahk
the evening	le soir	ler swahr
a fortnight	quinze jours	kanz zhoor
Good Friday	le Vendredi-Saint	ler vahndrerdee-san
half-an-hour	une demi-heure	ēun dermee-ērr
a holiday	un congé	un conzheh
an hour	une heure	ēun ērr
last month	le mois dernier	ler mwah dair-nee-eh
Lent	Carême m.	caraim'
Michaelmas	la Saint-Michel	la san-meeshel'
mid-day, noon	midi m.	meedee
mid-night	minuit m.	meenēuee
a minute	une minute	ēun meenēut'
a month	un mois	un mwah
the months	les mois	lai mwah
January	janvier	zhahn-v'yeh
February	février	fehv'ree-eh
March	mars	marss
April	avril	av-ree-y'
May	mai	mai
June	juin	zhēuan

English.	French.	Pronunciation.
July	*juillet*	zhēu-yai
August	*août*	oo
September	*septembre*	sep-tahn'br'
October	*octobre*	oc-tob'r'
November	*novembre*	novahn'br'
December	*décembre*	deh-sahn'br'
the morning	*le matin*	ler mat'an
the next day	*le lendemain*	ler lahnd'man
the night	*la nuit*	la nēuee
a quarter (3 months)	*un trimestre*	un treemaistr'
— of an hour	*un quart d'heure*	un karr' dērr
the seasons	*les saisons* f.	lai saizon
Spring	*le printemps*	ler pran-tahn
Summer	*l'été* m.	leh'teh
Autumn	*l'automne* m.	loh-ton
Winter	*l'hiver* m.	leevair
a second	*une seconde*	ēun sergond
sunrise	*le lever du soleil*	ler lev'eh dēu sol-ay'
sunset	*le coucher du soleil*	ler coo'sheh dēu sol-ay'
to-day	*aujourd'hui*	oh-zhoord'ēuee
to-morrow	*demain*	d'man
to-night	*cette nuit, ce soir*	set nēuee, ser swahr
this evening	*ce soir*	ser swahr
twilight	*le crépuscule*	ler creh-pēus-kēul
a week	*une semaine*	ēun s'main
Whitsuntide	*Pentecôte* f.	pahnt-coht
a year	*un an*	ern͡ahn
yesterday	*hier*	yair

Holidays in France   Jours fériés en France

All Saints' Day	*la Toussaint*	la too-san
Ascension Day	*l'Ascension* f.	lassahn's'yon
Assumption Day	*l'Assomption* f.	lassonp-s'yon
Christmas Day	*le jour de Noël*	ler zhoor der noh-el'
Easter Monday	*le lundi de Pâques*	ler lun'dee der pahk
Mid-Lent	*la mi-Carême*	la mee-caraim
National Fête	*la Fête Nationale*	la fait nah's'yon-ahl
New Year's Day	*le jour de l'an*	ler zhoor der lahn
Shrove Tuesday	*le mardi gras*	ler marr'dee grah
Whit-Monday	*le lundi de la Pentecôte*	ler lun'dee der la pahnt'coht

Italic *s* and *e* silent; thick n indicates nasal; apostrophe indicates suppressed vowel.

L'humanité; les parents Mankind; Relations

English.	French.	Pronunciation.
The aunt	*la tante*	la tahnt
a bachelor	*un célibataire*	un sellee-bat-air'
a boy	*un garçon*	un garson
a bride	*une mariée*	ēun mar-yeh'
a bridegroom	*un marié*	un mar-yeh'
the brother	*le frère*	ler frair
a brother-in-law	*un beau-frère*	un boh-frair
a child	*un enfant*	ern ahn-fahn
cousin	*cousin* m., *-e* f.	coozan', coozeen'
the daughter	*la fille*	la fee-y'
a daughter-in-law	*une belle-fille*	ēun bel-fee-y'
the family	*la famille*	la fam-ee-y'
the father	*le père*	ler pair
a father-in-law	*un beau-père*	un boh-pair
gentleman, sir	*monsieur*	mer-s-yēr
a gentleman	*un homme bien*	ern um b'yan ehlveh
a girl	*une fille* [*élevé*	ēun fee-y'
a grand-daughter	*une petite-fille*	ēun perteet-fee-y'
a grandfather	*un grand-père*	un grahn-pair
a grandmother	*une grand'-mère*	ēun grahn-mair
a grandson	*un petit-fils*	un p'tee-feess
the husband	*le mari*	ler maree'
a lady	*une dame*	ēun dahm
a man	*un homme*	ern um
the marriage	*le mariage*	ler marree-ahzh
the mother	*la mère*	la mair
a mother-in-law	*une belle-mère*	ēun bel-mair
the nephew	*le neveu*	ler n'vēr
the niece	*la nièce*	la nee-aiss
the orphan	*l'orphelin* m., *-e* f.	lor-f'lan, lor-f'leen
parents; relatives	*les parents* m.	lai parrahn
the sister	*la sœur*	la sērr
the sister-in-law	*la belle-sœur*	la bel-sērr
a son	*un fils*	un feess
a son-in-law	*un gendre*	un zhahndr'
an uncle	*un oncle*	ern oncl'
a widow	*une veuve*	ēun vērv
a widower	*un veuf*	un vērf
the wife, woman	*la femme*	la fam

Italic *e* and *s* silent; thick n indicates nasal; apostrophe indicates suppressed vowel.

The Human Body   Le corps humain (For Conversations see p. 141.)

English.	French.	Pronunciation.
The ankle	la cheville	la sher-vee-y'
the arm	le bras	ler brah
the back	le dos	ler doh
the beard	la barbe	la bar'b
the blood	le sang	ler sahn
the body	le corps	ler cor
the bones	les os m.pl.	laiz̑oh
the bowels	les entrailles f.pl.	laiz̑ahn-trah-ee-y'
the brain	le cerveau	ler sairvoh
the cheek	la joue	la zhoo
the chest	la poitrine	lah pwah-treen
the chin	le menton	ler mahnton
the ears	les oreilles f.pl.	laiz̑oh-ray'y'
the elbow	le coude	ler cood
the eye, the eyes	l'œil m., les yeux	ler-ee, laiz̑yer
the face	le visage	ler veezahzh
the fingers	les doigts m.pl.	lai dwah
the foot	le pied	ler p'yeh
the forehead	le front	ler fron
the hair	le cheveu	ler sh'ver
the hand	la main	la man
the head	la tête	la tait
the heart	le cœur	ler kerr
the kidneys	les reins m.pl.	lai ran
the knee	le genou	ler zh'noo
the leg	la jambe	la zhahnb
a limb	un membre	un mahn-br'
the lips	les lèvres f.pl.	lai laivr'
the liver	le foie	ler fwah
the lungs	les poumons m.pl.	lai poo-mon
the moustache	la moustache	la moostahsh
the mouth	la bouche	la boosh
the nails	les ongles m.pl.	laiz̑ongl'
the neck	le cou	ler coo
the nose	le nez	ler neh
the shoulders	les épaules f.pl.	laiz̑eh-pohl
the side	le côté	ler coh-teh
the skin	la peau	la poh
the spine	l'épine dorsale	leh-peen dor-sal'

English.	French.	Pronunciation.
the stomach	*l'estomac* m.	lestom-ah
the throat	*la gorge*	la gorzh
the thumb	*le pouce*	ler pooss
the toe	*l'orteil* m.	lohr-tay
the tongue	*la langue*	la lahng'
the tooth	*la dent*	la dahn
the whiskers	*les favoris* m.pl.	lai fav-or-ee
the wrist	*le poignet*	ler pwahnyai

Bodily & Mental Powers; Physical Qualities
Pouvoirs du corps et de l'esprit; qualités physiques

Age (of persons)	*âge* m.	ahzh
art	*l'art* m.	lahr
the beginning	*le commencement*	ler commahnssmahn
the bottom	*le fond*	ler fon
the character	*le caractère*	ler caractair
the dimensions	*les dimensions*	lai deemahn-s'yon
the breadth,	*la largeur*	la lahr'zhērr
the depth [width	*la profondeur*	la profon'dērr
the height	*la hauteur*	la hoh-tērr
the length	*la longueur*	la lon'ghērr
the thickness	*l'épaisseur* f.	leh-pai-sērr
the emotions (feel-	*les émotions* f.	laiz eh-moh-s'yon
anger [ings*)	*la colère*	la col-air
dislike	*l'aversion* f.	lah-vair-s'yon
envy	*l'envie* f.	lahnvee
hatred	*la haine*	la hain
pleasure	*le plaisir*	ler plaizeer
surprise	*la surprise*	la seūr-preez
the end	*le bout*	ler boo
the feelings	*les sentiments* m.	lai sahn-tee-mahn
foolishness, folly	*la folie*	la follee
gentleness	*la douceur*	la doo-sērr
goodness	*la bonté*	la bon-teh
greatness	*la grandeur*	la grahn-dērr
honesty	*l'honnêteté* f.	lonnait'erteh
honour	*l'honneur* f.	lonnērr
an idea	*une idée*	eūn^eedeh'
intelligence	*l'intelligence* f.	lan-tellee-zhahnss
judgment	*le jugement*	ler zhēuzh-mahn

* See also under "Religious Terms," p. 71.

English.	French.	Pronunciation.
knowledge	*le savoir*	ler sav-wahr
laughter, laughing	*le rire*	ler reer (*not* ree-er)
the middle	*le milieu*	ler mee-l'yĕr
the mind, intellect	*l'esprit* m.	less-pree'
patience	*la patience*	la pah-s'yahnss
reason (power of)	*la raison*	la raizon
the science	*la science*	la see-ahnss
the senses	*les sens* m.pl.	lai sahnss
feeling, touch	*le toucher*	ler toosheh
hearing	*l'ouïe* f.	lwee
seeing, sight	*la vision*	lah vee-z'yon
smell (-ing)	*l'odorat* m.	lodorah
taste, tasting	*le goût*	ler goo
the side	*le côté*	ler cohteh
smile, smiling	*sourire* m.	sooreer'
a sneeze	*un éternuement*	ern͡ et-air-neū'mahn
speaking, speech	*parole* f.	parrol
a speech (oration)	*un discours*	un deescoor
strength	*la force*	la furss
thinking, thought	*pensée* f.	pahn-seh'
the top	*le haut*	ler hoh
the voice	*la voix*	la vwah
weakness	*la faiblesse*	la faibless'
weeping	*les pleurs* m.	lai plĕrr
wisdom	*la sagesse*	la sahzh-ess'

Health   La santé

(For Conversations see p. 141.)

An accident	*un accident*	ern͡ acsee-dahn
the ambulance	*l'ambulance* f.	lahn-beūlahnss
appetite	*appétit* m.	appeh-tee
a bandage	*un bandage*	un bahndahzh
biliousness	*la bile*	la beel
a bite	*une morsure*	eūn morseūr
a blister	*une ampoule*	eūn ahnpool
a bruise	*une contusion*	eūn conteū-z'yon
a burn	*une brûlure*	eūn breūleūr
the chemist's (shop)	*la pharmacie*	la farr-ma-see [mahn
a chill	*un refroidisse-*	un rer-frwahd-eess-
cholera	*choléra* m. [*ment*	colleh-ra
a cold [tion	*un rhume*	un reūm
contagion, infec-	*contagion* f.	contahzh-yon

English.	French.	Pronunciation.
contagious, infec-	contagieux, -se	con-tahzh-yĕr, -yĕrz
the corn [tious	le cor	ler cohr
a cough	une toux	ēun too
the cramp	la crampe	la crahnp
deaf	sourd, -e	soor, soord
the dentist	le dentiste	ler dahnteest
diarrhœa	diarrhée f.	dee-arreh'
the diet	la diète	la dee-ait
the disease, illness	la maladie	la maladee
doctor, physician	médecin m.	med-san
the draught	la potion	lah poh-s'yon
dysentery	dysenterie f.	diss-ahn-tree
exercise	exercice m.	exairseess
exhausted, to be	être épuisé	aitr' en-pwee-zeh
the fainting	l'évanouissement	leh-vanweess'mahn
to faint (away)	s'évanouir [m.	seh-van'weer
the fever	la fièvre	la fee-aivr'
a fit	un paroxysme	un paroxeezm'
the fracture	la fracture	la fractēur
the gout	la goutte	la goot
headache	mal de tête m.	mal der tait
hoarseness	enrouement m.	ahnroo'mahn
the hospital	l'hôpital m.	loh'pee-tal
indigestion	indigestion f.	andee-zhes-t'yon
inflammation	inflammation f.	anflanmah's'yon
lame	boiteux, -se	bwahtĕr, -ĕrz
the medicine	la médecine	la med'seen
the nurse	la garde-malade	la gard-mal-ahd'
the ointment	l'onguent m.	lon-gahn
the pain	le mal	ler mal
paralysis	la paralysie	la paraleezee'
a pill	une pilule	ēun peelēul
the poison	le poison	ler pwah'zon
a poultice	un cataplasme	un cataplass-m'
the prescription	l'ordonnance f.	lohr-donahnss
quinine	quinine f.	keeneen'
the remedy	le remède	ler r'maid
rest	repos m.	rerpoh
a scald	une brûlure	ēun brēulēur
a scratch	une égratignure	ēun eg-rateen-yēur
the sea-sickness	le mal de mer	ler mal der mair

Italic s and é silent; thick n indicates nasal; apostrophe indicates suppressed vowel.

French Self-Taught   D

English.	French.	Pronunciation.
a sore throat	*un mal de gorge*	un mal der gohrzh
a sprain	*une entorse*	eun ahntohrss
a sting	*une piqûre*	eun peekeur'
a surgeon	*un chirurgien*	un sheereur-zh'yan
a symptom	*un symptôme*	un sanptohm
the temperature	*la température*	la tahnpeh-rat-eur
a clinical thermo-meter	*un thermomètre clinique*	un tairmomaitr' cleeneek'
a tonic	*un tonique*	un ton-eek'
the wound	*la blessure*	la bless'eur

Food, Drink, etc. Aliments, boissons, etc.

(For Game, Fish, etc., see p. 20; Vegetables and Fruits, p. 22; and for Conversations see pp. 110—116 and 130.)

The bill-of-fare, the bread [menu	*le menu*	ler merneu
	le pain	ler pan
bread, brown	*du pain bis*	deu pan bee
—, new, white	*— tendre, blanc*	deu pan tahndr', blahn
rolls	*des petits pains*	dai p'tee pan
bread and milk	*du lait chaud au*	deu lai shoh oh pan
a bun	*une brioche [pain*	eun breeohsh
butter	*du beurre*	deu berr
a cake	*un gâteau*	un gah-toh
cheese	*du fromage*	deu from-ahzh
cream	*de la crème*	d' la craim
a drink, beverage	*une boisson*	eun bwahsson
beer	*de la bière*	d' la b'yair
brandy	*du cognac*	deu kun-yak [oh
chocolate, cocoa	*du chocolat, cacao*	deu shoc-ol-ah, cac-ah-
claret	*du (vin de) Bor-*	deu (van der) bor-doh
coffee, black	*café (noir) [deaux*	deu caffeh (nwahr)
— with milk	*du café au lait*	deu caffeh oh lai
iced water	*de l'eau glacée*	d'loh glahsseh'
milk	*du lait*	deu lai
soda water	*de l'eau de seltz*	der loh d' selts
a siphon	*un siphon*	un seefon
wine (dinner)	*du vin ordinaire*	deu van ohrdeenair
— (red, white)	*— (rouge, blanc)*	deu van (roozh, blahn)
an egg; eggs	*un œuf; des œufs*	ern erf; daiz er'
the flour	*la farine*	la fareen
a fowl	*une volaille*	eun vol-ah'ee-y'
game	*gibier* m.	zheebyeh

Italic *e* and *i* silent; thick n indicates nasal; apostrophe indicates suppressed vowel.

English.	French.	Pronunciation.
grilled, boiled	grillé, -e	gree'yeh
honey	du miel	dēū m'yel
hunger; thirst	la faim; la soif	la fan; la swahf
the ice	la glace	la glahss
jam	de la confiture	d' la confeetēūr
marmalade	de la marmelade	d' la marrmer-lahd'
a meal	un repas	un rer-pah
meat	de la viande	d' la vee-ahnd
—, boiled	du bouilli	dēū boo'yee
—, roast	du rôti	dēū rohtee
bacon	du lard	dēū larr
beef	du bœuf	dēū bērf
—, roast	du rosbif	dēū rosbeef
beef-steak	du bifteck	dēū beeftek
calf's head	la tête de veau	la tait der voh
a chop, cutlet	une côtelette	ēūn coht-lett
a cut, slice	une tranche	ēūn trahnsh
the fat (meat)	le gras	ler grah
ham	du jambon	dēū zhahn-bon
a joint	une pièce	ēūn pee-aiss
kidneys	rognons m.	rohn-yon
lamb	de l'agneau	der lahn-yoh
the lean (meat)	le maigre	ler maigr'
the leg, haunch	la cuisse	la kēūeess
mince	du hachis	dēū hashee
mutton	du mouton	dēū mooton
pork	du porc	dēū pohr
a rib	une côte	ēūn coht
the round	la rouelle	la roo-ell
a shoulder	une épaule	ēūn ehpohl
the sirloin	l'aloyau	laloyoh
veal	du veau	dēū voh
mustard	de la moutarde	d' la mootar'd
oil	de l'huile f.	der lēūeel
pastry	de la pâtisserie	d' la pah-teess'ree
pepper	du poivre	dēū pwahvr'
rice	du riz	dēū ree
salt	du sel	dēū sel
sauce	de la sauce	d' la sohss
a sausage	une saucisse [m.	ēūn soh-seess
the seasoning	l'assaisonnement	lassaizunn'mahng

Italic r and é silent; thick n indicates nasal; apostrophe indicates suppressed vowel.

D*

English.	French.	Pronunciation.
smoke, to	*fumer*	feūmeh
an ash-tray	*un petit cendrier*	un p'tee sah**n**-dree-eh
a cigar	*un cigare*	un see-garr'
a cigarette	*une cigarette*	eūn seegaret'
a pipe (tobacco)	*une pipe*	eūn peep
tobacco	*du tabac*	deū tabah
the soup	*la soupe*	la soop
the stuffing	*la farce*	la farrss
the sugar	*le sucre*	ler seūkr'
— powdered	*— en poudre*	ler seūkr' ah**n** poodr'
under done	*saignant*	sainyah**n**
the vegetables	*les légumes* m.	la*i* leh-geūm
vinegar	*du vinaigre*	deū veenaigr'
well done	*bien cuit*	b'yan keūee

Cooking and Table Utensils
Ustensiles de cuisine et de table

(For "Shopping" see p. 120.)

A basin	*un bol*	un bol
the coffee pot	*la cafetière*	la caf-t'**yair**
the cork-screw	*un tire-bouchon*	un teer-boo-sho**n**
a cup	*une tasse*	eūn tass
the dish	*le plat*	ler pla (*as in* plat)
the dish-cover	*le couvre-plat*	ler coovrer-pla
a finger-bowl	*une rince-bouche*	eūn ranse-boosh
a fork	*une fourchette*	eūn foor-shett'
a glass, tumbler	*un verre*	un vair
a jug, pitcher	*une cruche*	eūn creūsh
the kettle	*la bouilloire*	la boo-ee-**wahr**
a knife	*un couteau*	un coo-toh
a lid	*un couvercle*	un coovair'cl'
the matches	*les allumettes* f.	laiz~alleūmett'
the milk-jug	*la crémière*	la craim-ya*i*r
the nut-crackers	*le casse-noisette*	ler cass-**nwahzett'**
the plate	*l'assiette* f.	lassyett'
the salt-cellar	*la salière*	la sal-ya*i*r
the sauce-bowl	*la saucière*	la sohss-ya*i*r
a saucer	*une soucoupe*	eūn soocoop'
the serviette	*la serviette* [*viette*	la sairvyett'
a serviette ring	*un rond de ser-*	un rond de*r* sa*i*rvyett'
the soup-ladle	*la cuillère à soupe*	la keūee-yair ah soop

Italic *r* and *é* silent; thick n indicates nasal; apostrophe indicates suppressed vowel.

English.	French.	Pronunciation.
a spoon	une cuillère	ēun kēuee-yair
an egg-spoon	une cuillère à œufs	ēun kēuee-yair ah ērf
a tea-spoon	une cuillère à thé	ēun kēuee'yair ah teh
a stove; gas —	un fourneau; — à	un foornoh; un foornoh
the table-cloth	la nappe [gaz	la napp [ah gahz
the tea-pot	la théière	la teh-yair
a tray	un plateau	un plat-oh
a water-bottle	une carafe	ēun carahf
a wine-glass	un verre à vin	un vair ah van

Les vêtements et la toilette — Dress and the Toilet

(See also p. 39, and for "Shopping," etc., see pp. 120—123.)

The bath	le bain	ler ban
the boots	les souliers m.	lai soolyeh
bootlaces	lacets de bottine	lassai d'botteen
the bracelet	le bracelet	ler brass-lai
the braces	les bretelles f.	lai bret-ell'
the brooch	la broche	la brosh
the brush	la brosse	la bross
a button-hook	un tire-bouton	un teer-booton
the buttons	les boutons m.	lai booton
the calico	le calicot	ler caleecoh
the cap (cloth)	la casquette	la cass-kett'
a cloak	un manteau	un mahntoh
the cloth (woollen)	le drap	ler drah
the clothes-brush	la brosse à habits	la bross ah ab-ee
a coat	un habit	ern ab'ee
the comb	le peigne	ler pain-y'
the cotton	le coton	ler co-ton
the dress	l'habit m.	lab'ee
evening dress	un frac	un frahk
the flannel	la flanelle	la flan-ell'
the fur	la fourrure	la foor-ēur
the garters	les jarretières f.	lai zharr'tyair
the gloves	les gants m.	lai gahn
the hair-pins	les épingles à che-	laiz ep-angl'ah sh'vēr
the hat, bonnet	le chapeau [veux f.	ler shap-oh
the jewellery	la bijouterie	la bee-zhoot'ree
the lace	la dentelle	la dahn-tell'
the linen	la toile	la twahl
the lining	la doublure	la doob-lēur

English.	French.	Pronunciation.
the looking-glass, mirror	le miroir	ler meer-wahr
the muslin	la mousseline	la mooss-leen'
a necktie	une cravate	eun cravat'
a needle	une aiguille	eun aigeuee-y'
an overcoat	un pardessus	un par-derseu
the parasol	l'ombrelle f.	lon-brell
the pins	les épingles f.	laiz ep-an'gl'
the pocket	la poche	la posh
a pocket-book	un porte-feuille	un pohrt'-fer-ee-y'
the purse	le porte-monnaie	ler port-monnai
a razor	un rasoir	un raz-wahr
the ribbon	le ruban	ler reubahn
a ring	une bague	eun bahg
the scissors	les ciseaux m.	lai seezoh
the sewing-cotton	le coton (à coudre)	ler co-ton (ah coodr')
the sewing-silk	la soie (à coudre)	la swah (ah coodr')
the shawl	le châle	ler shahl
a shoe-horn	un chaussepied	un shohss-p'yeh'
the shoes	les souliers m.	lai sool'yeh
the silk	la soie	la swah
the skirt	la jupe	la zheup
the sleeve	la manche	la mahnsh
the slippers	les pantoufles m.	lai pahn-too'fl'
the soap	le savon	ler sav'on
the spectacles	les lunettes f.	lai leun-ett'
the sponge	l'éponge f.	leh-ponzh
the stays, corset	le corset [mise)	ler cohr'sai
a stud	un bouton (de che-	un booton (der sh'meez)
the suit (of clothes)	l'habit complet	lab-ee conplai
the tape	la ganse	la gahnss
a thimble	un dé	un deh
the thread	le fil	ler feel
a tooth-brush	une brosse à dents	eun bross ah dahn
the trousers	le pantalon	ler pahntalon'
the umbrella	le parapluie	ler parapleuee'
the veil	le voile	ler vwahl
a waistcoat	un gilet	un zheelai
a walking-stick	une canne	eun cahnn'
a watch	une montre	eun mon-tr'
a waterproof coat	un imperméable	ern an-pair-meh-ahbl'

Italic r and i silent; thick n indicates nasal; apostrophe indicates suppressed vowel.

Liste de blanchissage　Washing List

(See Laundress, p. 124.)

English.	French.	Pronunciation.
Aprons, pinafores	*tabliers*	tab-lee-eh
blankets	*couvertures*	coovairteur
bodices	*corsages*	cohr-sahzh
bonnets, caps	*bonnets*	bonnai
chemises	*chemises*	sh'meez
collars (men's)	*cols*	col
— (ladies')	*collerettes*	col-rett'
—, lace	*— de dentelle*	col-rett' der dahn-tell'
combinations	*combinaisons*	con-bee-nai'zon
coverlets	*couvre-lits*	coovrer-lee
cuffs	*manchettes*	mahn-shett'
drawers, pairs of	*caleçons*	cal-son
dresses (gowns)	*robes*	rob
dressing-gowns	*peignoirs*	pain-wahr
— (morning)	*robes de chambre*	rob der shahnbr'
fronts	*chemisettes*	sh'meezett'
handkerchiefs	*mouchoirs*	moosh-wahr
—, silk	*— de soie*	moosh-wahr der swah
night-caps	*bonnets de nuit*	bonnai d' neuee
night-gowns, -shirts	*chemises de nuit*	sh'meez der neuee
pants (drawers)	*caleçons*	cal-son
petticoats	*jupons*	zheu-pon
—, flannel	*— de flanelle*	zheu-pon d' flan-el'
pillow-cases	*taies d'oreiller*	tay dohrai-yeh
serviettes	*serviettes*	sair-vee-et'
sheets	*draps* [me]	drah
shirts	*chemises (d'hom-*	sh'meez (dum)
sleeping-suits (pyjamas)	*vêtements de nuit*	vaitmahn d' neuee
socks, pairs of	*paires de chaus-*	pair der shoh-sett'
stockings, pairs of	*— de bas* [settes	pair der bah
—, silk, „	*— de bas de soie*	pair der bah d' swah
table-cloths	*nappes*	napp
towels	*essuiemains*	ess-euee-man
under-vests	*camisoles ; gilets de dessous*	cam-ee-zol ; zheelai der dessoo
waistcoats (flannel)	*gilets de flanelle*	zheelai d' flan-el'

Italic *s* and *t* silent; thick **n** indicates nasal; apostrophe indicates suppressed vowel.

The House & Furniture   La maison et les meubles
(For "Shopping" see p. 120.)

English.	French.	Pronunciation.
An armchair	un fauteuil	un fohter'ee
the ashes	les cendres m.	lai sahndr'
a basket	un panier	un pan'yeh
the bed	le lit [cher	ler lee
the bedroom	la chambre-à-cou-	la shahnbrah-coo'sheh
a bedstead	un bois de lit	un bwah d' lee
the bell, door-bell	la sonnette	la sonnett'
the blind	le store	ler stor
a book	un livre	un leevr'
a box	une boîte	eun bwaht
a brick	une brique	eun breek
the broom	le balai	ler bal-ai
the burner	le bec	ler bec
the candle	la chandelle	la shahndell'
a candlestick	un chandelier	un shahn-derl-yeh
the carpet, rug	le tapis	ler tap'ee
the ceiling	le plafond	ler plaf-on
the cellar	la cave	la cahv
a chair	une chaise	eun shaiz
the chamber utensil	le pot de chambre	ler poh d' shahnbr'
a chest of drawers	une commode	eun commod'
a clock	une horloge	eun ohr-lozh
the coals	le charbon de terre	ler sharr'bon der tair
the coal-scuttle	le panier	ler pan-yeh
the counterpane	la courtepointe	la coor-t'-pwant
a cupboard	une armoire	eun ar'mwahr'
the curtain	le rideau	ler ree'doh
a cushion	un coussin	un coossan'
the dining-room	la salle-à-manger	la sahllah-mahn'zheh
the door	la porte	la pohrt
the drawer	le tiroir	ler teerwahr
the drawing-room	le salon	ler sal-on
dresser (kitchen)	table de cuisine	tahbl' der keueezeen'
the electric light	la lumière électri-	la leumyair eh-lec-
a feather-bed	lit de plumes [que	lee d' pleum [treek'
the fender	le garde-cendre	ler garr'd-sahndr'
the fire	le feu	ler fer
the fire-wood	le bois à brûler	ler bwah ah breuleh
the flame	la flamme	la flam

English.	French.	Pronunciation.
a flat	*un appartement*	ern apparr-t'mahn
the floor	*le plancher*	ler plahnsheh
a footstool	*un tabouret*	un tab-oor-ai
the gas	*le gaz*	ler gahz
the grate	*la grille*	la gree-y'
the hall (entrance)	*le vestibule*	ler vesteebeül
a hearth-rug	*un tapis de foyer*	un tapee d' fwahyeh
incandescent	*incandescent*	ancahndessahn
the key	*la clef*	la cleh
the kitchen	*la cuisine*	la keüeezeen'
a lamp	*une lampe*	eün lahnp
the landing	*le palier*	ler pal'yeh
the larder	*le garde-manger*	ler gar'd-mahnzheh
the library	*la bibliothèque*	la beebleeoh-taik
the lock	*la serrure*	la serreür
the mattress	*le matelas*	ler mat'lah
the ornament	*l'ornement* m.	lornermahn
the passage, corri-	*le couloir*	ler coolwahr
the piano [dor	*le piano*	ler p'yahnoh
the picture	*le tableau*	ler tab'loh
a pillow	*un oreiller*	ern oh-rai-yeh
the poker	*le tisonnier*	ler tee-sonn'yeh
the roof	*le toit*	ler twah
the room	*la chambre*	la shahnbr'
a seat	*un siège*	un see-aizh
the shelf	*la tablette*	la tablett'
the shovel	*la pelle*	la pell
the sideboard	*le buffet*	ler beüffai
the smoke	*la fumée*	la feümeh'
the soot	*la suie*	la seüee
the staircase	*l'escalier* m.	less-cal'yeh
the stairs	*les escaliers*	laiz esscal-yeh
the switch	*le bouton*	ler booton
a table	*une table*	eün tabl'
the tongs	*les pincettes* f.	lai pansett'
a vase	*un vase*	un vahz
the wall	*le mur*	ler meür
a wash-hand-basin	*une cuvette*	eün keüvett'
the wash-stand	*la toilette*	la twahlett'
the window	*la fenêtre* [reau	la f'naitr'
a writing-desk	*un secrétaire, bu-*	un secrehtair, beüroh

Italic r and i silent; thick n indicates nasal; apostrophe indicates suppressed vowel.

Countries and Nations   Pays et nations

English.	French.	Pronunciation.
Africa	*Afrique* f.	afreek'
America	*Amérique* f.	am-ehreek'
an American	*un Américain*	ern͡ am-eh-ree-can
Asia	*l'Asie* f.	laz-ee
Australia	*l'Australie* f.	lohstral'ee
Austria	*l'Autriche* f.	loh-treesh
Belgium	*la Belgique*	la belzheek
Canada	*Canada* m.	canada
China	*la Chine*	la sheen
the Chinese	*les Chinois*	lai sheenwah
a country	*un pays*	un pai'ee
Denmark	*le Danemark*	ler dan-mar'k
the East Indies	*les Indes Orien-*	laiz͡ andz oree-ahntahl
the empire	*l'empire* m. [tales	lahnpeer
England	*l'Angleterre* f.	lahnglertair
the English	*les Anglais*	laiz͡ ahnglai
an Englishman	*un Anglais*	ern͡ ahnglai
Europe	*l'Europe* f.	lērrop
France	*la France*	la frahnss
the French	*les Français*	lai frahn'sai
a Frenchman	*un Français*	un frahn'sai
a German	*un Allemand*	ern͡ al'mahn
Germany	*l'Allemagne* f.	lal-mahn'y'
Great Britain	*la Grande Breta-*	la grahnd'brertahn-y'
Holland	*la Hollande* [gne	la hollahnd
India	*Inde* f.	and
Ireland	*l'Irlande* f.	leer-lahnd
an Italian	*un Italien*	ern͡ ee-tal'yan
Italy	*l'Italie* f.	lee-tal-ee
Japan	*le Japon*	ler zhap-on
the Japanese	*les Japonais*	lai͡ zhap-on-ai
the kingdom	*le royaume*	ler rwah'yohm
Russia	*la Russie*	la rēussee
a Russian	*un Russe*	un rēuss
Scotland	*l'Ecosse* f.	leh-coss
Spain	*l'Espagne* f.	less-pahn'y'
a Spaniard	*un Espagnol*	ern͡ ess-pahn'yol
Sweden	*la Suède*	la sēuaid
a Swiss	*un Suisse*	un sēueess

English.	French.	Pronunciation.
Switzerland	*la Suisse*	la séueess
Turkey	*la Turquie*	la teûr-kee
the United States	*les Etats-Unis*	laiz͡eh-tahz͡eûnee
the West Indies	*les Indes Occidentales*	laiz͡andz oxeedahntal

Villes, etc.   Towns, etc.

English	French	Pronunciation
Amiens	*Amiens*	ahmee-enn
Biarritz	*Biarritz*	beeahrritz
Boulogne	*Boulogne*	boolon'y'
Brittany	*La Bretagne*	la brertahn'y'
Brussels	*Bruxelles*	breû-sell'
Calais	*Calais*	cal'ai
Cannes	*Cannes*	cann'
Dieppe	*Dieppe*	dee-epp'
Dijon	*Dijon*	dee-zhon
Dover	*Douvres*	doo'vr'
English Channel	*La Manche*	la mahnsh
Fontainebleau	*Fontainebleau*	fontainbloh
Geneva	*Genève*	zhernaiv'
Havre	*Le Havre*	ler hahvr'
Hyères	*Hyères*	hee-air'
Loire, the	*La Loire*	lalwahr'
London	*Londres*	lon'dr'
Lyons	*Lyon*	lee'on
Marseilles	*Marseille*	mahr-sai'y'
Mediterranean, the	*La Mer Méditer-*	la mair med-ee-tair-
Mentone	*Menton* [*ranée*	mahnton [rah-neh'
Nice	*Nice*	neess
Nismes	*Nîmes*	neem
Normandy	*La Normandie*	la nohrmahndee'
Orleans	*Orléans*	ohrleh-ahn
Paris	*Paris*	parree
Rheims	*Reims*	ranss
Riviera, the	*La Rivière*	la reevee-air
Rochelle	*La Rochelle*	la roshell'
Rouen	*Rouen*	roo-ahn
Seine, the	*La Seine*	la sain
Straits of Dover	*Le Pas de Calais*	ler pah d' cal'ai
Toulon	*Toulon*	toolon'
Versailles	*Versailles*	vair-sah-ee-y'

Italic *r* and *i* silent; thick n indicates nasal; apostrophe indicates suppressed vowel.

Travelling by Rail and Road
Voyage en chemin de fer et en voiture

(For Conversations see pages 105—107.)

English.	French.	Pronunciation.
Apartments (suite	*un appartement*	ern appart'mahn
the arrival [of)	*l'arrivée* f.	larreeveh'
the bill	*la note*	la not
the boarding-house	*la pension*	la pahn-s'yon
the booking-office	*le guichet*	ler gheeshai
the "boots" (hotel)	*l'homme de peine*	lum der pain
the brake (on wheel)	*le frein*	ler fran
the bridle	*la bride*	la breed
the bus	*l'omnibus* m.	lomneebeuss
a cab	*un fiacre*	un feeah'kr'
a carriage	*une voiture*	eun vwah'teur
the chambermaid	*la femme de cham-*	la fam der shahnbr'
the cloak-room	*la consigne* [bre	la conseen-y'
the coachman	*le cocher*	ler cosh'eh
the coffee-room (in	*le café*	ler caf'eh
a cushion [hotel)	*un coussin*	un coossan
the custom-house	*la douane*	la doo-ahn'
customs officer	*douanier* m.	dwahn'yeh
the departure	*le départ* [voiture	ler deh-pahr [vwahteur
a drive	*une promenade en*	eun prom-nahd ahn
the engine	*la locomotive*	la locomoteev
excursion, trip	*excursion* f.	exkeurs'yon
—, to take an	*faire une —*	fair eun exkeurs'yon
the fare	*le prix de la place*	ler pree d' la plass
a foot-warmer	*un chauffe-pieds*	un shohf'pyeh
"Gentlemen"	"*Les hommes*"	laiz um
the guard	*le conducteur*	ler condeukterr
a guide	*un conducteur*	un condeukterr
a guide-book	*un guide*	un gheed
hall porter, door-	*le, la, concierge*	ler, la, con-s'yairzh
a hat-box [keeper	*un carton à cha-*	un carrton ah shap-oh
the hotel	*l'hôtel* m. [peau	loh-tel
the interpreter	*l'interprète* m.	lantairprait
"Ladies"	"*Les dames*"	lai dahm
the landlord, -lady	*le (la) propriétaire*	ler (la) propree-eh-tair'
the lavatory	*le cabinet de toi-*	ler cab'ee-nai dertwah-
lift, elevator	*ascenseur* m. [lette	assahnserr [lett'

Italic *r* and *i* silent; thick n indicates nasal; apostrophe indicates suppressed vowel.

English.	French.	Pronunciation.
lodgings, furnished	*chambres garnies*	shahnbr' gahrnee
the lost-property office	*le bureau des objets trouvés*	ler bēŭroh daiz obzhai trooveh
the luggage	*les bagages [gages*	lai bag-ahzh
the luggage-van	*le fourgon des bagagages*	lerfoorgon dai bagahzh
the manager	*le directeur*	ler deerektĕrr
the motor-car	*l'automobile*	lotomobeel'
a newspaper	*un journal*	un zhoornahl
the office	*le bureau*	ler bēŭroh
the ostler	*le garçon d'écurie*	ler gahr-son dehkĕŭree
a package	*un colis*	un col'ee
the payment	*le payement*	ler paimahn
the porter	*le commissionnaire*	ler commees-s'yonair'
— (railway)	*le facteur [naire*	ler fac'tĕrr
the railway	*le chemin de fer*	ler sh'man d' fair
—, tube [riage	*le tube*	ler tēŭb
the railway-car-	*le wagon*	ler vag'on
railway-station	*la gare*	la gahr
a receipt	*un reçu*	un rer-sēŭ
the reins	*les rênes*	lai rain
to ride (a horse)	*promener à cheval*	promneh ah sh'val
the riding-whip	*la cravache*	la cravahsh
the rug (travelling)	*la couverture de*	la coo'vairtĕŭr der
the saddle	*la selle [voyage*	la sell' [vwah-yahzh
the signal (railway)	*le signal*	ler seenyal
a sleeping-car	*un wagon-lit*	un vahgon-lee
the smoking-room	*le fumoir*	ler fēŭm-wahr
the station-master	*le chef de gare*	ler shef der gahr
a strap	*une courroie*	ēŭn coor-rwah
the subway	*le passage souterrain*	ler passahzh sooterran
the ticket	*le billet [rain*	ler bee'yai
first-class	*de première classe*	der prerm-yair class
return	*d'aller et retour*	dal'leh ai r'toor
a tip, gratuity	*un pourboire*	un poorbwahr
the train	*le train*	ler tran
the (electric) tram	*le tramway (élec-*	lertramwai(ehlectreek)
the trunk	*la malle [trique)*	la mall
the waiter	*le garçon*	ler gar'son
the waiting-room	*la salle d'attente*	la sahl dat-ahnt
a walk	*une promenade*	ēŭn prom-nahd
the whip	*le fouet*	ler foo-ai

Travelling by Sea   Voyage par mer

(For Conversations see page 159.)

English.	French.	Pronunciation.
Aft, after *adj.*	*de l'arrière*	der larr'yair
amidships *adj.*	*par le travers*	pahr ler travair
the anchor	*l'ancre* f.	lahn'cr'
a berth	*une cabine*	eūn cab-een'
the boat	*le bateau*	ler bat'oh
—, rowing	*— à rames*	ler bat'oh ah rahm
a boat-hook	*une gaffe*	eūn gaff'
the boatman	*le batelier*	ler bat-lee-eh
the boiler	*la chaudière*	la shohd'yair
the bow	*l'avant du vais-*	lav'ahn deū vessoh
the bridge (of ship)	*la passerelle* [*seau*	la pass'rell'
the buoy	*la bouée*	la boo-eh
—, bell-	*la bouée à cloche*	la boo-eh ah clohsh
the cabin	*la cabine*	la cab-een'
a cable	*un câble*	un cah'bl'
the captain	*le capitaine*	ler cap'ee-tain
the compass	*la boussole*	la boo-sol
the crew	*l'équipage* m.	leh-kee-pahzh
the deck	*le pont*	ler pon
—, lower	*le franc tillac*	ler frahn teeyac
—, upper	*le pont supérieur*	ler pon seūpeh-r'yĕrr
the deck-chair	*la chaise longue*	la shaiz long'
the dock	*le bassin*	ler bassan
—, dry	*le bassin d'échou-*	ler bassan deh-shoo-
to embark	*embarquer* [*age*	ahn-bar'keh [ahzh
the engineer	*l'ingénieur* m.	lan-zheh-n'yĕrr
the engine-room	*la chambre des machines*	la shahnbr' dai masheen
a fishing-boat	*un bateau de pêche*	un bat'oh d' paish
the fishing-net	*le filet*	ler feelai
the flag	*le pavillon*	ler pav-ee-yon
the fog-horn	*la sirène*	la seerain
fore *adj.*	*de l'avant*	der lavahn
the funnel	*la cheminée*	la shermeeneh
the gangway	*le passavant*	ler passavahn
the harbour, port	*le port*	ler porr
the helm, rudder,	*le gouvernail*	ler goo-vair-nah-ee
to land [wheel	*débarquer*	deh-bar'keh

Italic *r* and *é* silent; thick **n** indicates nasal; apostrophe indicates suppressed vowel.

English.	French.	Pronunciation.
the landing-stage	le débarcadère	ler deh-bar-cad-air'
leeward adj. & adv.	sous le vent	soo l' vahn
the life-belt	la ceinture de sauvetage [tage	la sahnteur der sohv-tahzh [tahzh
the life-boat	le bateau de sauve-	ler bat'oh der sohv-
the life-buoy	la bouée de sauve-	la boo-eh' d' sohvtahzh
the lighthouse	le phare [tage	ler fahr
the lightship	le bateau phare	ler bat'oh fahr
the mast	le mât	ler mah
the mate	le contre-maître	ler contr'-maitr'
an oar	une rame	eun rahm
the paddle-wheel	la roue à aubes	la roo ah ohb
the pier	la jetée	la zherteh
a pilot	un pilote	un peelott'
the port (side)	le bâbord	ler bahbor
the port-hole	le sabord	ler sah-bor
the pump	la pompe	la ponp
the quay	le quai	ler kai
a rope	une corde	eun cord
the sail	la voile	la vwahl
a sailing-ship	un navire à voiles	un naveer ah vwahl'
the saloon	le salon de pre-	ler salon der prerm-
screw (-propeller)	hélice f. [mière	eh-leess [yair
a seaman (sailor)	un matelot	un mat'loh
sea-sickness	le mal de mer	ler mal der mair
the ship	le navire	ler nav-eer'
signals, to make	donner des si-	donneh dai seenyoh
the sky-light	la lucarne [gnaux	la leucahrn'
the starboard (side)	le tribord	ler treebor
the steamboat	le bateau à vapeur	ler bat'oh ah vap'err
the steersman	le timonier	ler tee-mon'yeh
the stern	la poupe [vres	la poop
the steward	le commis des vi-	ler commee dai veevr'
stewardess	femme de chambre	fam der shahnbr'
the stoker	le chauffeur	ler shohferr
the tug	le remorqueur	ler rermorkerr
the ventilator	le ventilateur	ler vahntilaterr
the voyage	le voyage	ler vwah'yahzh
the watch (aboard ship)	le quart	ler kahr
windward adj.	du vent	deu vahn

Amusements   Divertissements

(For Conversations see p. 124.)

English.	French.	Pronunciation.
Admission, the charge for	le prix d'entrée	ler pree dahntreh
an aeroplane	un aéroplane	ern ah-ehroplahn
an air-ship	un (ballon) dirige-	un (bahllon) deereezh-
an aviator	un aviateur [able	ern ahveeahtĕrr [ahbl'
the ball	le bal [able	ler bal [zhahbl'
a balloon, dirigible	un ballon dirige-	un bahllon deeree-
the band, orchestra	l'orchestre m.	lor-kestr'
the cinematograph	le cinématographe	ler seenehmahtografh
a circus	un cirque	un seer'k'
a concert	un concert [-trice	un consair [-treess
the accompanist	l'accompagna-teur	lak-on-pahn-yah-tĕrr,
the chorus	le chœur	ler kĕrr
the conductor	le chef d'orchestre	ler shef dor-kestr'
a gramophone	un gramophone	un grahmofonn
the instruments	les instruments	laiz anstreŭmahn
—, brass	— de cuivre	— der keŭee'vr'
—, string	— à corde	— ah cord
the pianist	le pianiste	ler p'yan-eest
a piano	un piano	un p'yan-oh
the recital	le récit	ler reh-see
singer [sional	chanteur, -euse	shahn-tĕrr, -ĕrz
—, lady profes-	cantatrice	cahntatreess
a violin	un violon	un vee-ol-on
the entrance (door,	l'entrée f.	lahntreh
the exhibition [etc.	l'exposition f.	lex-poh-zee-s'yon
the exit	la sortie [ler	la sor-tee
a flying-machine	une machine à vo-	ĕun masheen ah voleh
games and pastimes	jeux et passetemps	zhĕrz ai pass'tahn
billiards	le billard [m.pl.	ler beeyar
boating	le canotage	ler canotahzh
chess	les échecs	laiz eh-shaïk
cricket	le cricket	ler creekaï
draughts	le jeu de dames	ler zhĕr der dahm
fishing	la pêche	la païsh
football	le foot-ball, or -bal	ler foot-bohl, or -bahl
golf	le golf	ler golf
golf-links	le terrain de golf	ler tair-ran der golf

English.	French.	Pronunciation.
games, *contd.*		
hunting	la chasse	la shass
the match	la partie (match)	la parr'tee (matsh)
the races	les courses f.	lai coorss
the enclosure	l'enclos m.	lahncloh
a jockey	un jockey	un zhokai
the racecourse	le champ de course	ler shahn der coorss
the race-horse	le cheval de course	ler sh'val der coorss
rowing, to row	ramer	rahmeh
shooting	le tir	ler teer
swimming	la natation	la nah-tah-s'yon
tennis	le tennis	ler tenneess
the grand stand	les tribunes m.	lai treebeūn
the music-hall	le café concert	ler caf'eh consair
the museum	le musée [bleaux	ler meūzeh'
the picture gallery	la galerie de ta-	la gal'ree der tabloh
reading-room	cabinet de lecture	cabeenai d' lecteūr
the subscription	la souscription	la sooscreep-s'yon
— (to periodicals)	l'abonnement m.	la-bon-mahn
the theatre	le théâtre	ler teh-ah'tr'
the act	l'acte m.	lact
the act-or, -ress	l'act-eur, -rice	lact'ĕrr, lactreess
the ballet	le ballet	ler ballai
the box-office	le bureau de loca-	ler beūroh der lohcah-
the cloak-room	le vestiaire [tion	ler vest-yair [s'yon
the curtain	le rideau	ler reedoh
the dancer	la danseuse	la dahnsĕrz'
the manager	le directeur	ler dee-rek-tĕrr
the opera	l'opéra m.	loh-peh-rah
the opera-glass	la lorgnette	la lornyett'
the play	la pièce	la p'yess
the programme	le programme	ler pro-grahm
the refreshment-	le buffet	ler beūffai
the scene [room	la scène	la sain
the seats	les places f.	lai plahss
the boxes	les loges f.	lai lozh
the dress-circle	le balcon de pre-	ler bal'con der prerm'-
the gallery	la galerie [mière	la gal'ree [yair
the pit	le parterre	ler parr'tair
reserved, stalls	les fauteuils m.	lai foh-ter-ee
the stage	la scène, le théâtre	la sain, ler teh-ah'tr'

Cycling   Cyclisme

(For Conversations see p.126.)

English.	French.	Pronunciation.
Acetylene	acétylène	asset'ee-lain
the axle	l'essieu, l'axe m.	less-yēr, lax
the ball-bearings	coussinets à bille	coosseenaiz͡ah bee-y'
the bearings	les coussinets m.	lai coosseenai
the bell	le grelot, la son- nette [cyclette	ler grerloh, la sonnett' [seek-lett'
a bicycle	un bicycle, une bi-	un bee-seekl', ēun bee-
a bolt	un boulon	un boolon
the brake	le frein	ler fran
caution	avis m.	av-ee
the cement	le ciment	ler see-mahn
the chain	la chaîne	la shain
the chain wheel	le grand pignon	ler grahn peenyon
the cone	le cône	ler cohn
the connection	le raccord	ler raccor
the crank	la manivelle [cles	la mah-nee-vel' [seekl'
cycle-maker	fabricant de bicy-	fabreekahn der bee-
cycle-race	course de bicycles	coorss der bee-seekl'
cycle-shop	magasin de —	magazan der bee-seekl'
cycling tour	voyage à bicyclette	vwah-yahzh ah bee-
the cycling-track	la piste	la peest [seeklett
a cyclist	un bicycliste	un } bee-seek-leest
— (lady)	une bicycliste	ēun }
a cyclometer	un compteur kilo-	un conterr keelohmeh'-
danger	danger [métrique	dahn'zheh [treek
to dismount	descendre de	des-sahndr' der
the dress-guard	le garde-jupe	ler garrd'-zhēup
to electro-plate	argenter	ar'zhahn'teh
the enamel	l'émail m.	leh-mah'ee
the foot-rest	le repos	ler rerpoh
the foot-step	le marche-pied	ler mar'sh-p'yeh
the fork	la fourche	la foorsh
the frame	le cadre	ler cad'r'
the friction	le frottement	ler frot'mahn [s'yon
gear, the	la multiplication	la mēulteepleecah-
—, a high	une grande multiplication	ēun grahnd mēultee- pleecah-s'yon
—, a low	une petite —	ēun perteet —

English.	French.	Pronunciation.
the gear-case	le garde-chaine	ler gar'der-shain
the gearing	l'engrenage m.	lahn-grer-nahzh
geared to	développé	deh-v'loppeh
the handles, grips	les poignées f.	lai pwahnyeh'
the handle-bar	le guidon	ler gheedon
the hub	le moyeu	ler mwah-yēr
the indiarubber	le caoutchouc	ler cah-oot-shoo'k
the inner tube	la chambre à air	la shahn-brah air
a knapsack	une valise	ēun val-eez
a lamp	une lampe	ēun lahnp
the lamp-bracket	le porte-lampe	ler pohrter-lahnp
the lamp-wick	la mèche [f.	la maish
lighting-up time	heure d'allumage	ērr dallēu-mahzh
a link	un maillon [m.	un mah'yon
lubricator	godet de graissage	go-dai der graissahzh
— protector	chapeau de — m.	shap-oh der graissahzh
the luggage-carrier	le porte-bagages	ler pohrt'-bag-ahzh
a map	une carte	ēun car't
to mount	monter	monteh
the mudguard	le garde-crotte	ler gar'd'-crott
a nut	un écrou, une vis	ern eh-croo, ēun veess
oil for burning	de l'huile à brûler	der lēueel ah brēuleh
— lubricating	— à lubrifier	der lēueel ah lēubree-
an oil-can	une burette	ēun bēurett [f'yeh
the outer-cover	l'enveloppe f.	lahn-v'lop'
the pedal	la pédale	la peh-dal
the pedal-rubber	le caoutchouc de	ler cah-oot-shoo'k der
the pump	la pompe [pédale	la ponp [peh-dal
the pump-tube	le raccord	ler rac-cohr
to pump up, inflate	gonfler	gon-fleh
rags	des chiffons	dai sheefon
removable	détachable	deh-tash-ahbl'
to repair	réparer [tion	reh-parreh [ah's'yon
the repairing outfit	la boîte à répara-	la bwaht ah reh-parr-
to ride a bicycle	aller à bicyclette	alleh ah bee-seeklett
the rim	la jante	la zhahnt
the saddle	la selle	la sell
the saddle-bag	le sachet de selle	ler sashai der sell
the saddle-pillar	la tige de selle	la teezh der sell
a screw	une vis, un écrou	ēun veess, ern eh-croo
to screw	visser	veesseh

Italic r and s silent; thick n indicates nasal; apostrophe indicates suppressed vowel.

E*

English.	French.	Pronunciation.
the screw-bolt of chain	le goujon d'assemblage	ler goozhon dassahn-blahzh
the screwdriver	le tourne-vis	ler toorn'-veess
the solution	la solution	la soleū-s'yon
a spanner	une clef [vitesse	eūn cleh [veetess'
the speed-gear	la disposition de	la deespozee-s'yon der
the spokes	les rayons m.	lai raiyon
the spring	le ressort	ler ressor'
to start	partir	par'teer
to steer	diriger	deereezheh
a strap	une courroie	eūn coor-rwah'
to take to pieces	démonter	deh-monteh
to tighten up	serrer	serreh
a toe-clip	une rattrape	eūn rat-rap'
a tricycle	un tricycle [lons	un tree-seekl'
trousers' clips	des pinces-pantalon	dai panss-pahn-tal-on
a tyre (pneumatic)	un pneu*	un pnĕr
to unscrew	dévisser	deh-veesseh
a valve	une valve [pape	eūn valv
the valve-cap	chapeau de soutube	shap-oh der soopap
the valve-tubing	tube de soupape	tēub der soopap
the wallet	la sacoche	la sacosh
the wheels	les roues	lai roo
the front wheel	la roue d'avant	la roo dav'ahn
the back wheel	— d'arrière	la roo darr-yair

Motoring   Automobilisme

(See also Cycling, p. 50, and Conversations, pp. 126—130.)

An accumulator	un accumulateur	ern akkeūmeūlah-tĕrr
a battery	une batterie	eūn batt'ree
the brake collar (steel)	la lame (ruban) de frein	la lahm (rēubahn) der fran
the cam	la came	la cam
the carburator	le carburateur	ler car'bēurat-ĕrr
the chain adjustment [tricity]	le tendeur de chaine [cité	ler tahndĕrr der shain [see-teh
to charge (with electricity)	charger d'électri-	sharrzheh deh-lec-tree-la
the claw	la griffe	la greeff
the contact breaker (trembler)	le trembleur	ler trahnblĕrr
cross-roads	carrefours m.	carr'foor

* Abbreviation of "un caoutchouc pneumatique."

English.	French.	Pronunciation.
the driver	le chauffeur	ler shoh-fĕrr
the driving pinion	le pignon de com-	ler peenyon der com-
an elbow	un coude [mande	un cood [mahnd
electric (-al)	électrique	eh-lec-treek
electricity	électricité f.	eh-lec-tree-see-teh
electric motor	moteur électrique	moh-tĕrr eh-lec-treek
to evaporate	évaporer	eh-vap-oh-reh
the exhaust	l'échappement m.	leh-shap-mahn
the exhaust-box	le silencieux	ler see-lahn-s'yĕr
(silencer)	[chappement	[mahn
the exhaust-valve	la soupape d'é-	la soo-pap deh-shap-
the feed-pump	la pompe d'ali-	la ponp dal-ee-mahn-
	mentation	tah-s'yon
to fill	remplir	rahnpleer
a flaw	une paille	ēun pah-ee-y'
the fly-wheel	le volant	ler volahn
a garage	un garage	un garahzh
the gas	le gaz	ler gahz
the generator	le générateur	ler zheh-neh-rah-tĕrr
the goggles	les lunettes	lai lēunett
the gradient [ing	la pente	la pahnt
the handle (start-	la manivelle	la man-ee-vell
the hooter, horn	le cor	ler corr
the horse-power	le cheval vapeur	ler sh'val vap-ĕrr
the ignition	l'allumage m.	lallēumahzh
the leakage	la fuite	la fēueet
the lever (handle)	le levier	ler lerv-yeh
the lever	la manette	la man-ett
to light (up)	allumer	al'lēumeh
the motor	le moteur	ler motĕrr
the packing	la garniture	la gahr'neetēur
petrol (some)	du pétrole	dēu peh-trol
pressure, high	haute pression f.	oht press'yon
—, low	basse pression	bahss press'yon
a rack	une crémaillère	ēun creh-mah-yair
the reservoir (tank)	le réservoir [ère	ler rezairvwahr
the reversing gear	la marche en arri-	la mar'sh ahn arryair
speed	la vitesse	la veetess'
—, full	toute vitesse	toot veetess'
—, high	grande vitesse	grahnd veetess'
—, low	petite vitesse	perteet veetess'

English.	French.	Pronunciation.
the speed-changing gear	le changement de vitesse	ler shahnzh-mahn der veetess'
the starting gear	la mise en marche	la meez͡ ahn mar'sh
the steering bar	le guidon de direc-	ler gheedon der deerec-
a tap	un robinet [tion	un rob-ee-nai [s'yon

Photography   Photographie

(For Conversations see p. 131.)

An amateur	un amateur	ern͡ am-at-ērr
backgrounds	des fonds, décors	dai fon, deh-cohr
backing	masquer	mahskeh
the bulging	le bombage	ler bon-bahzh
the burnisher	la presse à satiner	la press ah sat-ee-neh
a cameo portrait	l'épreuve bombée	leh-prērv bonbeh'
the camera bellows	la chambre à souf-	la shahnbr' ah soofflai
the cutting moulds	le calibre [flets	ler cal-ee-br'
a dark-room lamp	une lampe de labo-	ēun lahnp der labohr-
	ratoire, lanterne	at-wahr, lahntairn
a dark slide (double)	un châssis double	un shah-see doobl'
developing	le développement	ler deh-v'lopp'mahn
a dipper	un crochet	un crosh-ai
a dipper plate-clip	une pince	ēun panss
dishes	des cuvettes f.	dai kēuvett'
the draining rack	le séchoir	ler seh-shwahr
dry plates	des plaques sèches	dai plak sehsh
the enlargement	l'agrandissement	lag-rahn-deess-mahn
exposure	exposition f. [m.	expo-zee-s'yon
—, over	sur-exposé m.	sēur-expohzeh
—, snap	cliquet m.	cleekai
—, time	cliché, posé	cleesheh, pohzeh
—, under	sous-exposé	sooz͡ expohzeh
to fade	s'effacer, jaunir	seffasseh, zhohneer
the film side	la couche sensible	la coosh sahn-seebl'
the fixing	le fixage	ler feexahzh
a flash-light	un éclair magné-	ern͡ ehclair mahn-yeh-
the focus	le foyer [sique	ler fwah-yeh [zeek
the focussing	la mise au point	la meez oh pwan
the focussing-glass	la loupe	la loop
a funnel	un entonnoir [duée	ern͡ ahntonnwahr [eh
a glass measure	une mesure gra-	ēun merzēur grad-ēu-

English.	French.	Pronunciation.
half-length	*portrait mi-corps*	pohrtrai mee-cor
a half-plate	*une demi-plaque*	ēun der'mee-plak
a half-tone	*une demi-teinte*	ēun der'mee-tant
the intensifying	*le renforcement*	lerrahn-fohrss'-mahn
an iris diaphragm	*un diaphragme*	ēun deeafragmeereess
the lens	*l'objectif* m. [*iris*	lob-zhec-teef
—, the cap of	*le bouchon*	ler booshon
—, portrait	*l'objectif double*	lob-zhec-teef doobl'
the mount, -ing	*le collet* [*lage*	ler collai
mounting roller	*rouleau pour col-*	rooloh poor collahzh
a negative	*un cliché négatif*	un cleesheh negahteef
negatives on paper	*papier pelliculaire*	pap-yeh pelleekēulair
the photographer	*le photographe*	ler fotograhf
plate-holder	*châssis à plaques*	shah-see ah plak
platinotype	*platine* m. [m.	plat-een
positive bath	*bain positif* m.	ban poziteef
print mounter	*rouleau à épreuves*	rooloh ah eh-prērv
printing	*impression* f. [m.	anpress'yon
the printing frame	*le châssis presse*	ler shahsee press
the prints	*les épreuves* f.	laiz ehprērv
a quarter-plate	*un quart de plaque*	un karr' der plak
the shutter	*le volet*	ler voh-lai
—, instantaneous	*l'obturateur in-* *stantané*	lob-tēu-rat-ērr an-stahn-tah-neh
—, time	*— à pose*	lob-tēu-rat-ērr ah pohz
the silver bath	*le bain d'argent,* *sensibilisateur*	ler ban dar'zhahn, sahn-seebeeleezatērr
the speed indicator	*le marqueur auto-* *matique*	ler mar'kērr oh-toh-mat-eek
a spirit-level	*un niveau d'eau à* *bulle d'air*	un neevoh doh ah bēul dair
a spot, stain	*une tache*	ēun tash
a squeegee	*un rouleau* [*chouc*	un rooloh
—, india-rubber	*raclette* f. *en caout-*	raklett ahn ca-oot-
the swing-back	*la bascule*	la baskēul [shoo'
the toning bath	*le bain de virage*	ler ban der veerahzh
the varnishing	*le vernissage*	ler vairneesahzh
view-finder	*viseur, iconomètre*	veezērr, eeconomaitr'
a vignetting board	*un dégradateur*	un deh-grad-at-ērr
the washing rack	*le panier laveur*	ler pan-yai lav-ērr
— tank	*la cuve à lavage*	la kēuv ah lav-ahzh

Post, Telegraph and Telephone
Poste, télégraphe et téléphone

(For Conversations see page 123.)

English.	French.	Pronunciation.
Book-post, by	comme imprimés	kom anpreemeh'
called for, to be	poste restante f.	posst restahnt'
the collection	la levée	la l'veh'
the contents [tion	le contenu [douane	ler cont'neū [dooahn
customs declara-	déclaration f. à la	declarah-s'yon ah la
to deliver [ters)	distribuer	deestree'beū-eh
the delivery (let-	la distribution	la deestreebeū-s'yon
the description	la description	la derscreep-s'yon
the destination	la destination	la desteenah-s'yon
the excess postage	le surplus d'af-	ler seūrpleū daf-frahn-
	franchissement	sheess'mahn
the insured value	la valeur assurée	la val-ērr asseūreh'
the letter-box	la boîte aux lettres	la bwaht oh let'tr'
a letter-card	une carte-lettre	eūn carrt'-let'tr'
letter-post	poste aux lettres	posst oh let'tr'
a money order [per	un mandat-poste	un mahndah-posst
a newspaper wrap-	une bande timbrée	eūn bahnd tanbreh'
a parcel, packet	un paquet [colis	un pak'ai
parcel post	poste des petits	posst dai p'tee col'ee
postage paid	affranchi, -e	af-frahn'shee
a postal order	un bon de poste	un bon d' posst
a (picture) post-card	une carte-postale	eūn carrt'-posstal
	(illustrée)	(eelleūstreh)
the postman	le facteur (de la	ler fac'tērr (der la
	poste) [postes	posst)
the postmaster	le receveur des	ler rerss'vērr dai posst
the post-office	le bureau de poste	ler beūroh d' posst
to register (letter)	recommander	rercommahn'deh
reply-paid	réponse payée	reh-ponss pai-yeh'
a stamp	un timbre-poste	un tanbr'-posst
to telegraph	télégraphier	tel-eh-graf-yeh
the telegraph	la forme pour télé-	la form poor tel-eh-
form [senger	graphier [graphe	graf'yeh [graf
telegraph mes-	messager du télé-	messahzheh deū tel-eh-
— office	bureau m. du —	beūroh deū tel-eh-graf
a telegram	un télégramme	un telehgram
—, wireless	un radiogramme	un rahdiogram

English.	French.	Pronunciation.
telegraphy, wireless	*radiographie* f.	rahdiohgrafee
to telephone	*téléphoner*	tel-eh-foh'neh
engaged	*occupé*	okkeūpeh
to ring up	*sonner*	sonneh
telephone call-office	*bureau du télé-phone*	beūroh deū tel-eh-fon
telephone num-ber	*numéro de télé-phone*	neūmehroh der tel-eh-fon
the weight	*le poids*	ler pwah
weight, over	*l'excès de poids*	lexai' der pwah
—, under	*le manque de poids*	ler mahnk der pwah

La correspondance   Correspondence

(For Conversations see p. 135.)

The address	*l'adresse* f.	lad-ress'
to address	*adresser*	addresseh
to re-address	*— de nouveau*	ad-resseh der noovoh
blotting-paper	*papier buvard*	pap'yeh beūvahr
to copy, take a copy	*prendre copie*	prahndr' copee
the date	*la date*	la dat
the enclosure	*le contenu*	ler cont'neū
an envelope	*une enveloppe*	eūn ahn-v'lop
a fountain-pen	*une plume à réser-*	eūn pleūm ah rez'air-
immediate	*très pressé* [*voir*	trai press'eh [vwahr
the ink	*l'encre* f.	lahn'cr'
an inkstand	*un encrier*	ern ahn'cree-eh
a letter	*une lettre*	eūn let'tr'
a note	*un billet*	un bee'yai
the paper	*le papier*	ler pap'yeh
a pen (nib)	*une plume*	eūn pleūm
the pencil	*le crayon*	ler crai'yon
a penholder	*un porte-plume*	un pohrt'-pleūm
a penknife	*un canif*	un caneef
a quire	*une main*	eūn man
the seal	*le cachet*	ler cash-ai
the sealing-wax	*la cire à cacheter*	la seer ah cash'teh
a sheet (of paper)	*une feuille*	eūn fer-ee'y'
the signature	*la signature*	la seenyateūr
typewriter	*machine* f. *à écrire*	mash-een ah ehcreer
to type (-write)	*dactylographier*	dactilografyeh
typist	*dactylographe* m.f.	dactilograf
the writing	*l'écriture* f.	leh'cree-teūr

Professions and Trades   Professions et métiers

(For "Shopping" see p. 120.)

English.	French.	Pronunciation.
An artist	un artiste	ern͡ ar-teest'
an author, -ess	un auteur, une femme auteur	ern͡ ohtĕrr, ēun fam ohtĕrr
a baker	un boulanger	un boolahn'zheh
a banker	un banquier	un bahnk'yeh
a barber	un barbier	un bar'b-yeh
a bookbinder	un relieur	un rerlee-ĕrr
a bookseller	un libraire	un leebrair'
a brewer	un brasseur	un brass'ĕrr
a butcher	un boucher	un boo'sheh
a carpenter	un charpentier	un shar-pahn-t'yeh
a cashier	un caissier	un caiss'yeh
a chemist	un pharmacien	un far-mah-s'yan
a clerk	un commis	un commee
a cook	un cuisinier	un kĕueezeen'yeh
a draper [paper)	un marchand de nouveautés	un marshahn-d' noovoh-teh
an editor (news-	un rédacteur	un red-ac-tĕrr' [veel
an engineer, civil	un ingénieur civil	ern͡ anzhehnyĕrr see-
a fishmonger	un poissonnier	un pwah-son-yeh
a florist	une fleuriste	ēun flĕrreest'
a fruiterer, green-	un fruitier	un frĕueet'yeh
a glazier [grocer	un vitrier	un vee'tree-eh
a goldsmith	un orfèvre	ern ohr-faivr'
a governess	une gouvernante	ēun goovairnahnt'
a grocer	un épicier	ern͡ eh-peess'yeh
a hair-dresser	un coiffeur	un kwahff'ĕrr
a hatter	un chapelier [bas	un shap-erl-yeh
a hosier	un marchand de	un marshahn-d' bah
a jeweller	un bijoutier	un bee-zhoot-yeh
lady's maid	femme de chambre	fam der shahnbr'
a merchant	un négociant	un neh-goh-s'yahn
a messenger	un messager	un messah'zheh
a miller	un meunier	un mĕrn'yeh
a milliner	une modiste	ēun modeest'
a nurse (maid)	une bonne	ēun bunn
a pastry-cook	un pâtissier	un pah-teess'yeh
a physician, doctor	un médecin	un med-san
a policeman	un gendarme	un zhahn-dar-m'

English	French	Pronunciation
a porter, doorkeep- [er	un portier	un pohrt-yeh
a printer	un imprimeur	ern anprimērr
a professor	un professeur	un prof-ess-ērr
a provision-dealer	un marchand de comestibles	un mar-shahn der comesteebl'
a publisher	un éditeur	ern^editērr'
a saddler	un sellier	un sel'yeh
a servant, domestic	un (-e) domestique	un (eūn) domesteek
a shoe-black	un décrotteur	un dehcrottērr
a shoemaker	un cordonnier	un cohr-don'nyeh
a smith	un forgeron	un fohr-zher-ron
a stationer	un papetier	un pap-ert-yeh
a tailor	un tailleur	un tah-yērr
tobacconist	débitant de tabac	deb-bee-tahn der tab- [bah
a tradesman	un marchand	un mar'shahn
a watchmaker	un horloger	ern^ohr-lozh'eh
a workman	un ouvrier	ern^oov-ree-eh

Termes de commerce — Commercial Terms

(For Conversations see p. 141.)

Account, an	un compte	un cont
—, to close	pour fin de compte	poor fan der cont
—, current	compte courant	cont coorahn
—, joint	compte en partici- pation [vente	cont ahn par'teesee- pah-s'yon [vahnt
— of sale	compte rendu de	cont rahn-dēu der
—, on	pour le compte	poor ler cont
—, to settle an	solder un compte	sol-deh un cont
an accountant	un comptable	un con-tahbl'
an acknowledgment	un accusé	ern^ac-kēuzeh
an advance	des avances f.	daiz^avahnss
to advertise	faire de la publi-	fair der la pēubleesee-
an advertisement	une annonce [cité	eūn^annonss [teh
advice, a letter of	une lettre d'avis	eūn lettr' dav-ee
the agent	l'agent m.	lah-zhahn
an agency	une agence	eūn^azhahnss
apprentice	apprenti, -e	apprahn-tee
an arrangement	un arrangement	ern^arrahnzh-mahn
in arrears	en arrière	ahn^arryair
the assets	l'actif m.	lak-teef
assistant, shop	garçon de comptoir	garr-son der contwahr

English.	French.	Pronunciation.
assistant, shop (fe- at sight [male]	demoiselle de à vue [comptoir	der-mwah-zel der cont- ah veū [wahr
at three months	à trois mois	ah trwah mwah
an authorization	une autorisation	eūn͡ohtohreezah-s'yon
to authorize	autoriser	ohtohreezeh
the average	l'avarie f.	lav-ar-ee
the balance	le solde	ler sol'd'
to balance	balancer	balahnseh
the balance-sheet	le bilan	ler beelahn
the bank	la banque	la bahnk
the bank rate	le cours (d'escomp-	ler coor (desscont)
bankrupt, insolvent	en faillite [te	ahn fah-yeet
bankruptcy	faillite f.	fah-yeet
the bearer	le porteur	ler portērr
a berth, situation	une place	eūn plahss
a bill	un billet	un bee'yai
— of lading	un connaissement	un connaiss'mahn

bonded goods,
   goods in bond
	marchandises à
	   l'entrepôt
		marr'shahndeez͡ah
		   lahntrerpoh

book-keeper	teneur de livres	ter-nērr der leevr'
brokerage	courtage m.	coortahzh
business	affaires f.pl.	affair
the buyer	l'acheteur m.	lash'tērr
the cargo	la cargaison	la carr-gaizon
carriage (of goods)	le transport	ler trahnspor
carriage-paid	port payé	por pai-yeh
cash	argent m.	arr'zhahn
— account	compte de caisse	cont der caiss
— balance	encaisse f.	ahncaiss
—, for	au comptant	oh contahn
the catalogue	le catalogue	ler catalog
the charter	la charte	la sharr't
the charterer	l'affréteur m.	laffreh-tērr
the charter-party	la charte partie	la sharr'ter parr'tee'
a cheque	un chèque	un shaik
a claim	une réclamation	eūn rehclam-ah-s'yon
—, to send in	faire une „	fair eūn „

the clearing-house
   (banks)
	le comptoir de
	   règlement
		ler contwahr der rai-
		   glermahn

a clerk [stock	un commis	un commee
company, joint-	compagnie f.	con-pahn-yee

English.	French.	Pronunciation.
company, limited	compagnie limitée	con-pahn-yee leemee-
the contract, agree-	le contrat	ler contrah [teh'
to contract [ment	traiter	traiteh
the contractor	le contractant	ler contractahn
cost, insurance and	prix, assurance et	pree, asseūrahnss ai
freight (c.i.f.)	fret	frai
a creditor	un créancier	un creh-ahnss-yeh
the counting-house	la comptabilité	la contahbeeleeteh
the custom-house	la douane	la dwahn
customs duty	droit de douane	drwah der dwahn
damages, compen-	dommages et inté-	dommazh zaianteh-rai,
sation	rêts, compensation	conpahnsah-s'yon
debit and credit	débit et crédit	deh-bee ai creh-dee
a debt	une dette [trice f.	eūn dett [treess
debtor	débiteur m., débi-	deh-bee-tērr, deh-bee-
a declaration	une déclaration	eūn deh-clarrah-s'yon
to deliver (goods)	livrer	leevreh
delivery (of goods)	la livraison	la leevraizon
delivered free	rendu à domicile	rahndeū ah dommee-
	franc de port	seel frahn der por
demurrage	indemnité pour	andem-nee-teh poor
	surestarie	seū-ress-tarr-ee
department shop)	rayon m.	rai-yon
deposit (bank)	versement m.	vairs'mahn
— (part payment)	arrhes f.	ahrr'
a director	un directeur	un deerectērr
discount	escompte m.	esscont
to discount	escompter [dende	essconteh [dahnd
dividend warrant	coupon de divi-	coopon der deevee-
double-entry	tenue (f.) des livres	terneū dai leevr' ahn
	en partie double	pahr'tee doobl'
a draft, bill	une traite	eūn trait
to draw upon	tirer	teereh
the drawee	le tiré, la tirée	ler teereh, la teereh'
the drawer [bour	le tireur [lage	ler teerērr
dues, dock and har-	droits de mouil-	drwah der moo-yahzh
duty, liable to	soumis à des droits	soomeez˘ah dai drwah
— -free	franco de droits	frahn-coh der drwah
—, the export	le droit d'exporta-	ler drwah dexpohrtah-
	tion [tion	s'yon [s'yon
—, the import	le droit d'importa-	ler drwah danpohrtah.

Italic r and i silent; thick n indicates nasal; apostrophe indicates suppressed vowel.

English.	French.	Pronunciation.
enclosed (herewith)	ci-inclus	see-ancleū
enclosure (in letter)	un contenu	un contnēū
to endorse	endosser	ahndosseh
the endorsee	le porteur	ler portērr
the endorser	l'endosseur m.	lahndossērr
the endorsement	l'endos m.	lahndoh
an estimate	un devis	un dervee'
to estimate	donner un devis	donneh un dervee'
the exchange	bourse, change f.	boorrss, shahnzh
export (-ation)	exportation f.	expohrtah-s'yon
to export	exporter	expohrteh
the exporter	l'exportateur m.	lexpohrtat-ērr
exports	marchandises ex-	marr'shahndeez͡ex-
the firm	la maison [portées	la maizon [pohrteh'
forwarding	expédiant	ex-peh-d'yahn
free on board(f.o.b.)	franco à bord	frahn-co ah bor
a guarantee	une garantie	ēūn garrahn-tee
gross weight	poids brut	pwah brēūt
to import	importer	anporrteh
an importer	un importateur	ern͡anporrtat-ērr
imports	importations f.pl.	anporrtah-s'yon
information [come	renseignement m.	rahnsainyer-mahn
insolvent, to be-	faire faillite	fair fahyeet
an instalment	un versement par-	un vairss'mahn pahr-
insurance	assurance f. [tiel	assēūrahnss [s'yel
— policy	police d'assurance	poleess dassēūrahnss
— premium	prix (m.) „	pree dassēūrahnss
— rates	taxe (taux) d'assu-	tax (toh) dassēūrahnss
— underwriter	assureur [rance	assēūrērr
to insure	assurer	assēūreh
interest, rate of	taux de l'intérêt	toh der lan-teh-rai
introduction	présentation f.	preh-zahn-tah-s'yon
introduction, letter	lettre de recom-	lettrer der rercom-
of	mandation f.	mahn-dah-s'yon
the invoice	la facture	la factēūr
a lease	un bail	un bah-ee
lessee	locataire à bail	locatair ah bah-ee
lessor	bailleur, -euse	bah-ee-yērr, -yērz
liquidation	liquidation f.	leekeedah-s'yon
to load	charger	sharr'zheh
the loss	la perte	la pairt

English.	French.	Pronunciation.
the manager	le gérant	ler zheh-rahn
the market	le marché	ler marr'sheh
the market-day	le jour de marché	ler zhoor der marr'sheh
market price	cours du marché	coor dēu marr'sheh
the money market	la bourse	la boorrss
negotiable	négociable	neh-goss-yahbl'
—, not	non-négociable	non-nehgoss-yahbl'
net (nett)	net	net
number (of house)	numéro m.	nēumehroh
the office	le bureau	ler bēuroh
an order	une commande	ēun commahnd
to order	commander	commahndeh
payable	payable	pai-yahbl'
a payment	un payement	un pay-mahn
prepaid	affranchi	affrahnshee
the price	la cote	la cot
—, cost	le prix coûtant	ler pree cootahn
— -list [sale	— courant	— coorahn
—, trade, whole-	— de gros	— der groh
prohibited goods	marchandises f.pl. prohibées	mar'shahndeez pro-ee-beh'
a quotation	une cote	ēun cot
a receipt	un reçu	un rersēu
a reduction	une réduction	ēun reh-dēuk-s'yon
to register	enregistrer	ahn-reh-zhees-treh
registered letter	lettre chargée (recommandée)	lettrer shahr'zheh' (rercommahndeh' [treh'
registered tonnage	jauge enregistrée	zhohzh ahnrehzhees-
registration	enregistrement	ahn-reh-zhees-trer-
a remittance	une remise	ēun rermeez [mahn
the rent	le loyer [gramme	ler lwahyeh [leh-gram
reply by telegram	réponse f. par télé-	reh-pohnss par' teh-
the representative	le représentant	ler rer-preh-zahn-tahn
retail, adj.	en détail	ahn deh-tah-ee
the salesman	le marchand	ler marr'shahn
the secretary	le secrétaire	ler sercrehtair
a settlement	un règlement	un raiglermahn
a shareholder	un-e actionnaire	ern (ēun) acs'yonnair
shares, ordinary	actions f.	acs'yon
—, preference or debenture	obligations f.	ohbleegah-s'yon

Italic r and i silent; thick n indicates nasal; apostrophe indicates suppressed vowel.

English	French.	Pronunciation.
to ship	embarquer	ahnbarr'keh
shipper	expéditeur	expeh-dee-tĕrr
shipping charges	frais de charge-	frai der shar-zher-
solvent	solvable [ment	solvahbl' [mahn
stock (of goods)	marchandises (f.)	mar'shahndeez ahn
	en magasin	magazan
— (security)	fonds publics m.	fon peubleek
— -broker	agent de change	azh-ahn der shahnzh
— -taking	inventaire m. [que	anvahntair
telegraphic address	adresse télégraphi-	ad-ress tehlehgraffeek
the towing charges	les frais de halage	lai frai der al-ahzh
trade, commerce	commerce m. [de	commairss
to trade (deal) in	faire le commerce	fair ler commairss der
traveller, commer-	commis voyageur	commee vwahyahzhĕrr
a trustee [cial	un fidéi-commis-	unfeedeh-ee-commees-
— in bankruptcy	un syndic [saire	un sandeek [sair
unloading	déchargement m.	deh-shar'zhermahn
a warehouse	un magasin	un magazan
wholesale, adj.	en gros	ahn groh
wharf	le quai	ler kai
wharfage	quayage m.	kai-yahzh

Legal Terms   Termes judiciaires

(For Conversations see p. 143.)

English	French.	Pronunciation.
Acquittal	acquittement m.	akkeett'mahn
an action, law-suit	un procès	un prossai
an affidavit	une déclaration	eun deh-clarah-s'yon
the agreement	la convention	la convahns'yon
an allegation	une allégation	eun alleh-gah-s'yon
to allege	alléguer	alleh-gheh
to arbitrate	arbitrer	ahrbeetreh
arbitration	arbitrage m.	ahrbeetrahzh
an arrangement	un arrangement	ern arrahnzh-mahn
to arrest	arrêter	arraiteh
to attest	attester	attesteh
attestation	attestation f. [reur	attestah-s'yon
an attorney	un avoué, procu-	ern av-weh,prokeurĕrr
attorney, power of	procuration f.	prokeurah-s'yon
to authorize	autoriser	ohtohreezeh
the award	le jugement	ler zheuzh-mahn
to award	décerner	deh-sairneh

English.	French.	Pronunciation.
bail	*caution* f.	coh-s'yon
a barrister, counsel	*un avocat*	ern avvocah
a bond (for loan)	*une obligation*	eun ohbleegah-s'yon
the case	*la cause*	la cohz
charge (accusation)	*accusation* f.	akkeuzah-s'yon
to charge	*accuser*	akkeuzeh
the claimant	*le réclamant*	ler reh-clamahn
a client	*un-e client-e*	un cleeahn, eun clee-
complainant	*plaignant-e*	plainyahn, -t [ahnt
the conviction	*la condamnation*	la condahnah-s'yon
a court of justice	*un tribunal*	un treebeunal
criminal	*criminel-le*	cree-mee-nel
decision (of a case)	*résolution* f., *juge-ment final*	reh-zoleu-s'yon, zheuzh-mahn feenal
a deed	*un titre*	un teetr'
the defence	*la défense*	la deh-fahnss
to defend	*défendre*	deh-fahn-dr'
defendant	*défend-eur, -eresse*	deh-fahnd-err, -ress
the depositions	*les dépositions* f.	lai deh-pozee-s'yon
the discharge	*l'acquittement* m.	lakit'mahn
equity	*(en) équité*	(ahn) eh-kee-teh
the evidence	*l'évidence* f.	leh-vee-dahnss
execute a deed, to	*signer un contrat*	seenyeh un contrah
execution (of deed)	*exécution* f.	ex-eh-keu-s'yon
executor	*exécuteur* m.	ex-eh-keu-terr
fee (of office)	*honoraire* m.	on-ohrair
fine (payment)	*amende* f.	ahmahnd
the fraud	*la fraude* [m.	la frohd
imprisonment	*emprisonnement*	ahnpreez-on'mahn
an information	*une dénonciation*	eun deh-nons'yah-s'yon
informer	*délateur, dénon-ciateur*	deh-laterr, deh-non-see-ah-terr
an injunction	*une injonction*	eun an-zhonk-s'yon
an inventory	*un inventaire*	ern an-vahn-tair
the jail	*la geôle, prison*	la zhohl, preezon
the judge	*le juge*	ler zheuzh
judgment	*jugement* [ment	zheuzh-mahn [mahn
—, to give	*prononcer un juge-*	prononseh un zheuzh-
jurisdiction	*juridiction* f.	zheureedeek-s'yon
the jury	*le jury*	ler zheuree
justice; in-	*justice* f.; *in-*	zheusteess; an-

English.	French.	Pronunciation.
the law	*la loi*	la lwah
lawful, legal	*légal*	leh-gal
a lawyer, solicitor	*un avoué*	ern av-weh
magistrate (police)	*juge d'instruction*	zhĕuzh danstrĕuc-s'yon
oath, to take an	*prêter serment*	praiteh sairmahn
the pardon	*le pardon*	ler pahr'don
the parties	*les parties* f.	lai pahrtee
penal	*pénal*	peh-nal
perjury	*parjure* m.	pahr'zhĕur
petitioner	*pétitionnaire* m.f.	peh-teess-yonnair
the plaintiff	*le demandeur*	ler dermahndĕrr
police-station	*poste* m. (*de police*)	posst (der poleess)
— officer	*agent de police*	azhahn d' poleess
the procedure	*la procédure*	la pro-seh-dĕur
the proof	*la preuve*	la prĕrv
prosecution	*poursuite* f.	poor-sĕueet
prosecutor, -trix	*poursuivant-e*	poor-sĕueevahn, -t
the punishment	*la punition*	la pĕunee-s'yon
the robbery	*le vol*	ler vol
the seal	*le sceau*	ler soh
to seal (deed, &c.)	*sceller*	selleh
sentence	*sentence* f.	sahntahnss
service (of writ)	*signification* f.	seen-yeefeecah-s'yon
to sign	*signer*	seen-yeh
statement (written)	*exposé (écrit)* m.	expozeh (eh-cree)
a statute	*un statut*	un statĕu
statutory	*statutaire*	statĕutair
to sue	*poursuivre*	poorsĕueevr'
suit, trial	*procès* m.	prossai
summons	*assignation* f.	asseen-yah-s'yon
a surety	*un garant*	un garrahn
the tenant, *m.f.*	*le (la) locataire*	ler (la) lok-ah-tair
the testator	*testat-eur, -rice*	testat-ĕrr, -reess
the theft	*le vol*	ler vol
the thief	*le voleur*	ler volĕrr
under seal	*sous seing* m.	soo san
unlawful, illegal	*illégal*	eelleh-gal
valid, invalid	*valide ; invalide*	val-eed ; an-val-eed
the will (testament)	*le testament*	ler test-am-ahn
the witness	*le témoin*	ler teh-mwan
a writ	*une assignation*	ĕun͡ asseenyah-s'yon

English.	Grades, titres, etc. French.	Ranks, Titles, etc. Pronunciation.
Council; -lor	*conseil; -ler*	consay'; consay'yeh
the Crown	*la couronne*	la coo-runn'
a deputy	*un député*	un deh-pēu-teh
duke; duchess	*duc; duchesse*	dēuk; dēushess'
earl, count; count-	*comte; comtesse*	cont'; contess'
the Emperor [ess	*l'empereur*	lahnp'rērr'
the Empress	*l'impératrice*	lanpehrahtreess'
the Government	*le gouvernement*	ler goovairn'mahn
the heir; heiress	*l'héritier; l'héri-*	lehreet'yeh; lehreet'-
His, Her Majesty	*Sa Majesté* [tière	sa mahzhesteh [yair'
His, Her Royal	*Son Altesse*	son ahltess' rwahyahl
Highness	*Royale*	
the King; Queen	*le roi; la reine*	ler rwah; la rain
Mayor; Mayoress	*Maire; femme du-*	mair; fam dēu mair
the Minister	*le ministre*	ler meeneestr'
the Ministry	*le ministère*	ler meeneestair'
the Nobility	*la noblesse*	la nobless'
Parliament	*le parlement*	ler pahr-ler-mahn
the Presidency	*le présidence*	ler prehzeedahnss
the President,	*le président*	ler prehzeedahn
chairman		
Prince, Princess	*prince; princesse*	pranss; pransess'
the Royal Family	*la Famille Royale*	la famee-y' rwahyahl'
the secretary	*le secrétaire*	ler sercrehtair'
the senator	*le sénateur*	ler sen-ah-tērr
the Throne	*le trône*	ler trohn
the treasurer	*le trésorier*	ler trezoryeh

Naval and Military Titles
Titres navals et militaires

The adjutant	*l'adjudant*	lad-zhēu-dahn
the admiral	*l'amiral*	lammeeral
the boatswain	*le contre-maître*	ler contrer-maîtr'
the brigadier	*le général de bri-*	ler zheh-neh-ral der
the bugler	*le clairon* [gade	ler clairon [bree-gad
the captain	*le capitaine*	ler cap-ee-tain
the chaplain (army)	*l'aumônier*	loh-mohn-yeh
chief of the staff	*chef d'état-major*	shef deh-tah-mazh-orr
the colonel	*le colonel*	ler collonel

Italic *r* and *s* silent; thick n indicates nasal; apostrophe indicates suppressed vowel.

F*

English.	French.	Pronunciation.
the colour-serjeant	le sergent-major	ler sairzhahn-mazhorr
the commandant	le commandant	ler commahn-dahn
the commander-in-chief [officer	le commandant-en-chef [dant	ler commahn-dahn ahn-shef [dahn
the commanding	l'officier comman-	loffeess'yeh commahn-
a corporal	un caporal	un cap-oh-ral
a doctor	un docteur	un doc-tērr
a drummer	un tambour	un tahnboor
an engineer	un soldat du génie	un soldah dēu zhehnee'
a field-marshal	un maréchal (de France)	un marreh-shahl (der frahnss)
a general	un général	un zheh-neh-ral
a lieutenant	un lieutenant	un l-yērt'nahn
a major	un major [rine	un mazh-orr
a marine	un soldat de ma-	un sol-dah der marreen
the mate	le second lieute-nant [marine	ler s'gon l-yērt'nahn [marreen
a midshipman	un aspirant de	ern aspeerahn der
a nurse	un infirmi-er, une	ern an-feerm-yeh, ēun
an officer	un officier [-ère	ern offeess'yeh [-yair
the orderly	l'ordonnance	lordonnahnss
the orderly officer	l'officier d'ordon-	loffeess'yeh dordon-
the paymaster	le trésorier [nance	ler trez-or-yeh [nahnss
the pilot	le pilote	ler peelott
a private	un simple soldat	un san-pler sol-dah
the quartermaster	le quartier-maitre	ler kahrt'yeh-mai'tr'
a sailor, bluejacket	un marin	un marran
a sergeant	un sergent [major	un sairzhahn [mazh-orr
a staff officer	un officier d'état-	ern offees'yeh dehtah-
a trumpeter	un trompette	un tronpett
warrant-officer	maître d'équipage	maitrer deh-kee-pahzh

Naval and Military Terms
Termes navals et militaires

The ambulance	l'ambulance f.	lahnbēulahnss
ammunition	munitions de guerre	mēunee-s'yon der gair
an army corps	un corps d'armée	un cor dahr'meh'
the artillery	l'artillerie f.	lahr'tee-yer-ree
the band	la musique	la mēuzeek

Italic *s* and *i* silent; thick n indicates nasal; apostrophe indicates suppressed vowel.

English.	French.	Pronunciation.
the barracks	la caserne	la caz-airn
a battalion	un bataillon	un bat-ah-ee-yon
a battery	une batterie	eūn bat'ree
a battle	une bataille	eūn bat-ah-ee-y'
a bayonet	une baïonnette	eūn bah'yonnett
a brigade	une brigade	eūn breegahd
a bugle	un clairon	un clairon
the camp	le camp	ler cahn
the cannon, gun	le canon	ler can-on
the cartridge	la cartouche	la cahr'toosh
the cavalry	la cavalerie	la cav-al'ree
cease fire!	cessez le feu!	sesseh l' fēr!
the colours (of a regiment)	le drapeau (du régiment)	ler drap-oh (dēu reh-zhee-mahn)
— (of a ship)	le pavillon	ler pav-ee-yon
the column	la colonne	la col-onn
the commissariat	le commissariat	ler com-eess-sahr-yah
the court-martial	le conseil de guerre	ler consay der gair
the crew (navy)	l'équipage	leh-kee-pahzh
a defaulter	un délinquant	un deh-lan-kahn
the defence	la défense	la deh-fahnss
a detachment	un détachement	un deh-tashmahn
the discipline	la discipline	la deesseepleen
to dismiss (from service)	renvoyer du service [cheval	rahn-vwah-yeh dēu sairveess
to dismount	descendre de	der-sahndrer der sh'val
the dockyard	l'arsenal maritime	lahr-s'nal marreeteem
to drill	faire l'exercice	fair lexairseess
the drum	le tambour	ler tahnboor
duty, on	de service	der sairveess
embarkation; dis-	em-barquement;	ahn-bahr-k'mahn; deh-
the enemy	l'ennemi m. [dé-	len'mee
the engagement	le combat	ler conbah
the enlistment	l'enrôlement m.	lahn-rohl-mahn
the entrenchment	le retranchement	ler rertrahnsh-mahn
the equipment	l'équipement m.	leh-keep-mahn
the escort	l'escorte f.	less-cohrt
the expedition (military)	l'expédition militaire f.	lex-peh-dee-s'yon meeleetair
fatigue duty	la corvée	la corveh'
a field day	un jour d'exercice	un zhoor dexairseess

English.	French.	Pronunciation.
field exercises	des exercices de campagne	daiz exairseess der cahnpahnyer
— glass, a	une lorgnette	eun lorn-yet [yer
— gun	pièce de campagne	pee-aiss der cahnpahn-
— hospital, a	un hôpital de camp	ern ohpeetal der cahn
file, in single	à la file	ah la feel
the flag	le drapeau	ler drapoh
the flank	le flanc	ler flahn
the fleet	la flotte	la flott
the formation	la formation	la fohrmah-s'yon
the fort	le fort	ler fohr
to fortify	fortifier	fohrteefee-eh
furlough, on	en congé	ahn con-zheh
the garrison	la garnison	la gahr'neezon
guard, the advance	l'avant-garde f.	lav-ahn-gahr'd
—, the rear	l'arrière-garde f.	larreeair-gahr'd
a gunner	un canonnier	un cannonnee-eh
the head-quarters	le quartier-général	ler kahrt'yeh-zhehneh-
infantry	l'infanterie	lanfahnt'ree [ral
—, mounted	— montée	— monteh'
the Intelligence Department	le service des renseignements	ler sairveess dai rahn-sainyermahn
an ironclad	un vaisseau cui-	un vaissoh keuee-ras-
a knapsack	un havresac [rassé	ern ahv-rersak [seh
a lance	une lance [leurs	eun lahnss
the line of fire	la ligne des tirail-	la leenyer dai teerah-
the manœuvre	la manœuvre	la manervr' [ee-yerr
man-of-war	vaisseau de guerre	vaissoh der gair
military service	service militaire	sairveess meeleetair
the mine	la mine	la meen
to muster	faire l'appel	fair lappell
non-combatant	non combattant	non conbattahn
the parade	la parade	la parrahd
a patrol	une patrouille	eun patroo-ee-y'
a picket	un piquet [guerre	un peekai [gair
a prisoner of war	un prisonnier de	un preezonn-yeh der
the quarters	les quartiers m.	lai kahr't-yeh
rank and file	sous-officiers, caporaux et soldats	sooz-offeessyeh, kah-porohz ai soldah
the rations	les rations f.	lai rah-s'yon
a recruit	une recrue	eun rer-creu

English.	French.	Pronunciation.
a regiment	*un régiment*	eūn reh-zhee-mahn
the regulations	*les règlements* m.	lai raiglermahn
a rifle	*un fusil*	un feū-zee
the salute	*le salut*	ler saleū
the scout	*l'éclaireur* m.	leh-clairērr
the sentry	*la sentinelle*	la sahnteenell
the shell [ball]	*la bombe, l'obus* m.	la bonb, lohbeūss
the shot (cannon-	*le boulet*	ler boolai
to skirmish	*escarmoucher*	esscahr'moosheh
a soldier	*un soldat*	un soldah
a spy	*un espion*	ern͡essp'yon
a squadron (mil.)	*un escadron*	ern͡esscahdron
—, (naval)	*une escadre*	eūn͡esscahdr'
the staff (military)	*l'état-major*	lehtah-mazhorr
a submarine (boat)	*un (bateau) sous-*	un (bat-oh) soo-marran
a sword	*une épée* [*marin*	eūn͡eh-peh
a torpedo-boat	*un torpilleur*	un tohr-pee-yērr
transport (ship)	*vaisseau de trans-*	vaissoh der trahns-
the trenches	*les tranchées* [*port*	lai trahn-sheh' [por
the troops	*les troupes* f.	lai troop
the uniform	*l'uniforme* m.	leūneeform
wing, the left	*l'aile gauche* f.	lail gohsh
—, the right	„ *droite* f.	„ drwaht
the wounded	*les blessés*	lai blesseh

Termes de religion Religious Terms

(For Conversations see p. 139.)

Absolution	*absolution* f.	absoleū-s'yon
the aisle	*l'aile* f.	lail
the altar	*l'autel* m.	lohtel
the angel	*l'ange* m.	lahnzh
the baptism	*le baptême*	ler bah-taim
the bible	*la Bible*	la beebl'
the bible society	*la société biblique*	la sohs-yeh-teh beeb-
belief, faith	*foi* f.	fwah [leek
a breviary	*un bréviaire*	un brehv-yair
the burial	*l'enterrement* m.	lahn-tairmahn
the cathedral	*la cathédrale*	la cah-teh-drahl
the cemetery	*le cimetière*	ler seem-t'yair
the chapel	*la chapelle*	la shapell
charity	*charité* f.	sharreeteh

Italic r and é silent; thick n indicates nasal; apostrophe indicates suppressed vowel.

English.	French.	Pronunciation.
the choir	le chœur	ler kĕrr
Christian	chrétien, -ne	creht-yan, -yenn
—, a	un-e chrétien-ne	un —, eūn creht-yenn
Christianity	christianisme m.	creestee-ahn-eezm'
a church	une église	eūn eh-gleez
a clergyman	un ecclésiastique	ern eh-cleh-zee-asteek
—, (Protestant)	ministre, pasteur	meeneestr', pastĕrr
—, (Catholic)	curé, abbé	keūreh, abbeh
the Creator	le Créateur	ler creh-at-ĕrr
a creed	un credo	un cred-oh
divine	divin, -e	deevan, deeveen
divinity	divinité f.	deeveeneeteh
eternal life	vie éternelle f.	vee eh-tairnell
eternity	éternité f.	ehtairneeteh
everlasting	éternel, -le	eh-tairnel
faithful	fidèle	feedail
faithfulness	fidélité f.	feedeh-leeteh
fear	peur f.	pĕrr
to forgive	pardonner	pahr'donneh
forgiveness	pardon m.	pahr'don
God	Dieu	d'yĕr
the Gospel	l'évangile m.	leh-vahn-zheel
a grave	une fosse, tombe	eūn foss, tonb
Heaven	ciel m.	s'yell
Hell	enfer m.	ahnfair
holiness	sainteté f.	san-terteh
holy [nion	saint, -e [ment	san, sant
the Holy Commu-	le Saint Sacre-	ler san sacrermahn
the Holy Ghost	le Saint-Esprit	ler sant-espree
hope	espérance f.	esspehrahnss
a hymn-book	un livre d'hymnes	un leevr' deem-n'
Jesus Christ	Jésus-Christ	zheh-zeū-cree
joy	joie f.	zhwah
the lectern	le lutrin	ler leūtran
the litany	les litanies f.	lai leetahnee
the liturgy	la liturgie	la leeteūrzhee
the Lord	le Seigneur	ler sainyĕrr
love	amour m.	am-oor
marriage	mariage m.	marr-yahzh
mass, high	grand'messe } f.	grahn-mess
—, low	messe basse }	mess bahss

English.	French.	Pronunciation.
matins	les matines f.	lai mateen
mercy	miséricorde f.	meezehreekord
a missal	un missel	un meessel
the mission	la mission	la meess'yon
the missionary	le missionnaire	ler meess'yonnair
the nave	la nef	la nef
the offertory	l'offertoire m.	loffairt-wahr
the organ	les orgues f.	laiz̄ ohrg'
the organist	l'organiste m.	lohrganeest
peace	paix f.	pai
penance	la pénitence	la peh-neetahnss
praise	louange f.	l'wahnzh
to praise	louer	l'weh
to pray	prier	pree-eh
a prayer	une prière	eūn pree-air
a prayer-book	un livre de prieres	un leevr' der pree-air
to preach	prêcher	praisheh
the preacher	le prédicateur	ler preh-deecahtĕrr
a priest	un prêtre	un praitr'
a Protestant	un-e protestant-e	un protestahn, eūn -t
the pulpit	la chaire	la shair
to repent	se repentir	ser rerpahnteer
repentance	repentir m.	rerpahnteer
a Roman Catholic	un catholique	un catoleek
the sacrament	le sacrement	ler sacrermahn
sacred	sacré, -e	sacreh
the salvation	le salut	ler saleū
the Saviour	le Sauveur	ler sohvĕrr
the sermon	le sermon	ler sairmon
service	l'office	lof-feess
—, morning	„ du matin	„ deū matan
sin ; to sin	péché m. ; pécher	peh-sheh ; peh-sheh
sinful	coupable	coopabl'
sinner	péch-eur, -eresse	peh-shĕrr, peh-sh'ress
sorrow	chagrin m.	shagran
the soul	l'âme f.	lahm
to trust	se fier à	ser f'yeh ah
truth	vérité f.	veh-ree-teh
the verger	le sacristain	ler sacreestan
vespers	les vêpres f.	lai vaipr'
to worship	adorer	adohreh

Italic r and s silent ; thick n indicates nasal ; apostrophe indicates suppressed vowel.

Cardinal Numbers*   Nombres cardinaux

French.	Pronunciation.		French.	
1 *Un*	un		73 *soixante-treize*	
2 *deux*	dĕr		74 *soixante-quatorze*	
3 *trois*	trwah		75 *soixante-quinze*	
4 *quatre*	katr'		76 *soixante-seize*	
5 *cinq*	sank		77 *soixante-dix-sept*	
6 *six*	seess		78 *soixante-dix-huit*	
7 *sept*	set		79 *soixante-dix-neuf*	
8 *huit*	ēūeet		80 *quatre-vingts*	katr'-van
9 *neuf*	nĕrf		81 *quatre-vingt-un*	
10 *dix*	deess			[katr'-van-un
11 *onze*	onz		82 *quatre-vingt-deux*	
12 *douze*	dooz			&c.
13 *treize*	trayz		90 *quatre-vingt-dix*	
14 *quatorze*	katorz		91 *quatre-vingt-onze*	
15 *quinze*	kanz		92 *quatre-vingt-douze*	
16 *seize*	saiz			&c.
17 *dix-sept*	dee-set		100 *cent*	sahn
18 *dix-huit*	deez-ēūeet		101 *cent un*	sahn-un
19 *dix-neuf*	deez-nĕrf		110 *cent dix*	sahn-deess
20 *vingt*	van		120 *cent vingt*	sahn van
21 *vingt et un*	vant-ai-un		130 *cent trente*	
22 *vingt-deux*	vant-dĕr		200 *deux cents*	
23 *vingt-trois*	vant-trwah		300 *trois cents*	
24 *vingt-quatre*	vant-katr'		400 *quatre cents*	
25 *vingt-cinq*	vant-sank		500 *cinq cents*	san sahn
26 *vingt-six*	vant-seess		600 *six cents*	see sahn
27 *vingt-sept*	vant-set		700 *sept cents*	sai sahn
28 *vingt-huit*	vant-ēūeet		800 *huit cents*	ēūee sahn
29 *vingt-neuf*	vant-nĕrf		900 *neuf cents*	nĕr sahn
30 *trente*	trahnt		1,000 *mille*	meel
40 *quarante*	karrahnt		2,000 *deux mille*	
50 *cinquante*	sankahnt		3,000 *trois mille*	
60 *soixante*	swahssahnt		10,000 *dix mille*	dee meel
70 *soixante-dix*			20,000 *vingt mille*	
71 *soixante et onze*	swahssahnt		a million	*un million*
72 *soixante-douze*	[ai onz			[un meelyon

1911   Nineteen hundred and eleven   *Mil neuf cent onze*

* See "French Grammar Self-Taught," pp. 32-44.

Italic *r* and *s* silent; thick n indicates nasal; apostrophe indicates suppressed vowel.

	Les nombres ordinaux	Ordinal Numbers[*]
English.	**French.**	
First	*premier*	prerm-yeh
second	*second*	sergon
third	*troisième*	trwahz-yem
fourth	*quatrième*	katryem
fifth	*cinquième*	sank-yem
sixth	*sixième*	seez-yem
seventh	*septième*	sett-yem
eighth	*huitième*	eūeet-yem
ninth	*neuvième*	nĕrv-yem
tenth	*dixième*	deez-yem
eleventh	*onzième*	onz-yem
twelfth	*douzième*	dooz-yem
thirteenth	*treizième*	traiz-yem
fourteenth	*quatorzième*	katorz-yem
fifteenth	*quinzième*	kanz-yem
sixteenth	*seizième*	saiz-yem
seventeenth	*dix-septième*	deez-sett-yem
eighteenth	*dix-huitième*	deezeūeet-yem
nineteenth	*dix-neuvième*	deez-nĕrv-yem
twentieth	*vingtième*	vant-yem
twenty-first	*vingt et unième*	vant-ai-eūn-yem
twenty-second	*vingt-deuxième*	vant-dĕrz-yem
thirtieth	*trentième*	trahnt-yem
fortieth	*quarantième*	karrahnt-yem
fiftieth	*cinquantième*	sankahnt-yem
sixtieth	*soixantième*	swahssahnt-yem
seventieth	*soixante-dixième*	swahssahnt-deez-yem
eightieth	*quatre-vingtième*	katrer-vant-yem
ninetieth	*quatre-vingt-dixième*	katrer-van-deez-yem
hundredth	*centième*	sahnt-yem
thousandth	*millième*	meell-yem

Collective & Distributive Numbers, etc.
Nombres collectifs et distributifs, etc.

All	*tout*	too
a couple	*un couple*	un coopl'
double, two-fold	*double*	doobl'
a (or one) dozen	*une douzaine*	eūn doozain
a (one) fifth	*un cinquième*	un sank-yem

[*] See "French Grammar Self-Taught," pp. 35, 36.

Italic *s* and *i* silent; thick n indicates nasal; apostrophe indicates suppressed vowel.

English.	French.	Pronunciation.
firstly	*premièrement*	prerm-yair'**mahn**
a gross	*une grosse*	ēun gross
the half	*la moitié*	la mwaht-**yeh**
half-a-dozen	*une demi-dou-*	ēun dermee-doozai**n**
the last	*le dernier* [*zaine*	ler dairn-yeh
once	*une fois*	ēun fwah
one at a time	*un à la fois*	ē**rn**⌢ah la fwa**h**
one by one	*un à un*	ē**rn**⌢ah ē**rn**
a pair	*une paire*	ēun pair
a part, portion	*une partie*	ēun par-**tee**
a quarter, fourth	*un quart*	un karr
a score [*part*	*une vingtaine*	ēun vantai**n**
secondly	*secondement*	sergond'mah**n**
singly	*séparément*	seh-parreh-mah**n**
a third	*un tiers*	un t'yai**r**
thirdly	*troisièmement*	trwahz-yem'**mahn**
three-fold, treble	*triple*	treepl'
three-quarters	*trois quarts*	trwah **karr**
three-sevenths	*trois septièmes*	trwah sett-**yem**
twice	*deux fois*	dēr fwah
two at a time	*deux à la fois*	dērz⌢ah la fwa**h**
two by two	*deux à deux*	dērz⌢ah dē**r**

Adjectives* Adjectifs

English.	French.	Pronunciation.
Able; un-	*capable; in-* *de*	capahbl'; a**n**capahble**r**
active; in-	*actif; inactif*	acteef; een-acteef [de**r**
agreeable; dis-	*agréable; dés-*	ag-reh-ahbl'; dehzag-
angry	*fâché* [*agréable*	fahsheh [reh-ahbl'
anxious	*inquiet*	an-k'yeh
awkward	*maladroit*	maladrwa**h**
bad; — (of meat,	*mauvais; gâté*	moh-vai; gahteh
beautiful [&c.)	*beau*	boh
bitter	*amer*	amai**r**
blind	*aveugle*	avērgl'
blunt	*émoussé*	ehmoosse**h**
bold	*hardi*	ahr-dee
brave	*brave*	brahv
bright	*brillant*	bree-yah**n**
broad, wide	*large*	lahrzh
busy	*affairé*	affaireh

* For plural and feminine of adjectives see "French Grammar Self-Taught," pp. 16, 20.

English.	French.	Pronunciation.
calm	*calme*	cal-m'
careful	*soigneux*	swahn-yĕr
careless	*sans souci*	sahn soo-see
certain ; **un-**	*certain ; incertain*	sairtan ; **an**-sairtan
cheap	*bon marché*	bon marr-sheh
cheerful	*joyeux*	zhwah-yĕr
civil ; **un-**	*civil ; incivil*	seeveel ; **an**-seeveel
clean	*propre*	pro-pr'
clear	*clair*	clair
clever	*habile*	ah-beel
cold	*froid*	frwah
comfortable ; un- (of persons)	*à son aise ; mal à son aise*	ah son͡aiz ; mal ah son͡aiz
comfortable ; un- (of things)	*agréable ; désagréable*	ag-reh-ahbl' ; daiz-ag-reh-ahbl'
common ; un-	*commun ; peu —*	commun; pĕr commun
complete ; in-	*complet ; in-*	conpleh ; **an**-
content	*content*	contahn
continual	*continuel*	conteenĕuel
cool (weather, etc.)	*froid*	frwah
correct ; in-	*correct ; incorrect*	cohrrect ; **an**cohrrect
cruel	*cruel*	crĕu-el
curious	*curieux*	kĕur'yĕr
damp	*humide*	ĕumeed
dangerous	*dangereux*	dahn-zherrĕr
dark, gloomy	*sombre*	sonbr'
dead, deceased	*mort*	mor
deaf	*sourd*	soor
dear	*cher*	shair
deep	*profond*	profon
different	*différent*	deeffeh-**rahn**
dirty, nasty	*sale*	sahl
distinct	*distinct*	deesta**nkt**
dry	*sec*	sek
dull	*lourd*	loor
eager	*avide*	av-eed
early	*matinal, en avan-*	mateenal, ahn͡avahnss
easy (not difficult)	*aisé [ce*	aizeh
empty	*vide*	veed
equal ; un-	*égal ; inégal*	eh-gal ; een-eh-gal
every	*chaque*	shahk

English.	French.	Pronunciation.
fair, just	*juste*	zheŭst
false	*faux*	foh
famous	*fameux*	fam-ēr
fashionable; un-	*à la mode; pas à la*	ah la mod; pahz̑ ah la
fast (quick)	*vite* [*mode*	veet [mod
— (fixed)	*fixe*	feex
fat, stout	*gras*	grah
favourable	*favorable*	fav-oh-rahbl'
few	*peu de*	pēr der
fine (small, etc.)	*fin*	fan
fine (beautiful)	*beau*	boh
firm	*ferme*	fairm
fit; un-	*propre; inepte*	propr'; eenept
flat	*plat*	plah
foolish	*sot*	soh
fortunate; un-	*heureux; mal-*	er-rēr; mal-er-rēr
free	*libre*	leebr'
fresh	*frais*	frai
frequent	*fréquent*	freh-kahn
full	*plein*	plan
gay	*gai*	gai
general	*général*	zheh-neh-ral
generous	*généreux*	zheh-neh-rēr
gentle	*doux*	doo
glad	*content*	contahn
good	*bon*	bon
grand	*grand*	grahn
great	*grand*	grahn
handsome	*beau*	boh
happy; un-	*heureux; mal-*	er-rēr; mal-er-rēr
hard	*dur*	dēur
heavy	*pesant*	perzahn
high	*haut*	oh
hilly	*montagneux*	montahn-yēr
hollow	*creux*	crēr
honest	*honnête*	onnait
hot	*chaud*	shoh
ill	*malade*	mallahd
important; un-	*important; sans*	anportahn; sahnz
	importance	anportahnss
injurious	*injurieux*	an-zhēur'yēr

English.	French.	Pronunciation.
interesting ; un-kind (obliging)	intéressant; peu — obligeant	an-teh-ressahn ; pēr — oblee-zhahn
lame	estropié	esstrop-yeh
late	en retard	ahn re-tahr
light (as to weight)	léger	leh-zheh
little	petit	pertee'
long	long	lon
loose (untied)	délié	deh-l'yeh
loud	haut	oh
low (position)	bas	bah
many	beaucoup de	boh-coo der
mild (weather)	doux	doo
miserable	misérable	meezeh-rahbl'
modern	moderne	modairn
muddy	boueux	boo-ēr
narrow	étroit	eh-trwah
necessary ; un-new (not old)	nécessaire ; pas — neuf	neh-sessair ; pah — nērf
nice (to taste)	bon	bon
— (delightful)	joli	zholee
noble ; ig-	noble ; ignoble	nobl' ; eenyobl'
numerous	nombreux	nonbrēr
old	vieux	v'yēr
open	ouvert	oovair
ordinary ; extra-pale	ordinaire ; extra-pâle	ordeenair ; extra-pahl
patient ; im-perfect ; im-plain (clear)	patient ; im-parfait ; im-évident	passyahn ; an-pahrrfai ; an-eh-vee-dahn
— (intelligible)	intelligible	antellee-zheebl'
pleasant ; un-poisonous	agréable à; dés- à toxique	ag-reh-ahbl' ah ; dehz-toxeek [ag-reh-ahbl'ah
polite	poli	polee
poor	pauvre	pohvr'
possible ; im-practical	possible ; im-pratique	posseebl' ; an-prat-eak
present	présent	preh-zahn
pretty	joli	zholee
private	privé	preeveh
probable ; im-proud	probable ; im-fier	probahbl' ; an-f'yair

English.	French.	Pronunciation.
public	*public*	peūbleek
pure	*pur*	peūr
queer	*bizarre*	beezahrr
quick, rapid	*rapide*	rap-eed
quiet	*tranquille*	trahnkeel
rare	*rare*	rahrr
raw (uncooked)	*cru*	creū
ready (prepared)	*prêt*	pra*i*
real ; un-	*réel ; non réel*	reh-el ; non reh-el
reasonable ; un-	*raisonnable ; dé-*	raizonnahbl'; deh-
regular ; ir-	*régulier ; ir-*	reh-geūl-yeh ; eer-
reliable (news, etc.)	*sûr*	seūr
remarkable	*remarquable*	rermahrr'kahbl'
rich	*riche*	reesh
right (correct)	*juste*	zheūst
ripe	*mûr*	meūr
rough (in manners)	*grossier*	gross-yeh
— (uneven)	*raboteux*	rab-ot-ēr
round	*rond*	ron
rude	*impoli*	anpolee
rural	*champêtre*	shahn-pa*i*tr'
sad	*triste*	treest
safe	*sauf*	sohf
same	*même*	maim
satisfactory	*satisfaisant*	sat-eez-ferzahn
secure (safe)	*sûr*	seūr
serious	*sérieux*	seh-r'yēr
severe	*sévère*	seh-vair
sharp	*aigu*	a*i*geū
short	*court*	coor
silent	*silencieux*	seelahns'yēr
simple	*simple*	sanpl'
single (one)	*seul*	sērl
slight, unimportant	*peu important*	pēr anpohrtahn
soft (to touch, etc.)	*doux*	doo
solid	*solide*	sol-eed
sound (healthy)	*sain*	san
sour	*aigre*	a*i*gr'
square	*carré*	carreh
stormy	*orageux*	oh-rah-zhēr
straight	*droit*	drwah

English.	French.	Pronunciation.
strange	*étrange*	eh-trahnzh
strong	*fort*	fohr
stupid	*stupide*	steūpeed
sufficient; in-	*suffisant; in-*	seūffeezahn; an-
suitable	*convenable à*	conv'nahbl' ah
sure	*sûr*	seūr
sweet	*doux*	doo
tall (of persons)	*grand*	grahn
tender	*tendre*	tahndr'
terrible	*terrible*	tairreebl'
thick	*épais*	eh-pai
thin	*mince*	manss
tight (of clothes)	*étroit*	eh-trwah
tiresome (tedious)	*ennuyeux*	ahn-neūee-yĕr
tough (of meat)	*dur*	deūr
troublesome	*fâcheux*	fah-shĕr
true	*vrai*	vrai
ugly	*laid*	lai
unsettled (weather)	*variable*	vahrr'yahbl'
unsound (bad)	*gâté*	gahteh
urgent	*urgent*	eūr-zhahn
useful	*utile [commun*	eūteel [mun
usual; un-	*ordinaire; peu*	ohr-deenair; pĕr com-
valuable	*précieux*	preh-s'yĕr
various	*divers*	deevair
violent	*violent*	v'yolahn
visible; in-	*visible; in-*	veezeebl'; an-
warm	*chaud*	shoh
weak	*faible*	faibl'
well (fortunate)	*bien*	b'yan
wet	*mouillé*	moo-yeh
wholesome; un-(of	*sain; malsain*	san; malsan
wicked [food]	*méchant*	meh-shahn
willing; un-	*bien disposé;*	b'yan deespozeh;
wise	*sage [mal—*	sahzh [mal—
wonderful	*étonnant*	eh-tonnahn
wooden	*de bois, en bois*	der bwah, ahn bwah
worthless	*sans valeur*	sahn val-ĕrr
wretched	*malheureux*	mal-er-rĕr
wrong (erroneous)	*erroné*	airroneh
young	*jeune*	zhĕrn

Italic *s* and *i* silent; thick n indicates nasal; apostrophe indicates suppressed vowel.

Verbs* Verbes

English.	French.	Pronunciation.
To accept	accepter	aksepteh
„ admire	admirer	admeereh
„ answer	répondre	reh-pondr'
„ approve	approuver	ap-proo-veh
„ arrive	arriver	ar-ree-veh
„ ascend	monter	monteh
„ ask	demander	dermahndeh
„ assure	assurer	as-sēureh
„ awake	s'éveiller	seh-vai-yeh
„ be	être	aitr'
„ be able	pouvoir	poovwahr
„ be afraid	avoir peur [tre]	avwahr pērr
„ be angry (with)	être en colère (con-	aitr' ahn colair (contr')
„ be fine	faire beau	fair boh
„ be hungry	avoir faim	av-wahr fan
„ be ignorant of	ignorer	eenyohreh
„ be injurious	nuire à	nēueer ah
„ be mistaken	se tromper	ser tronpeh
„ be quiet, silent	se taire	ser tair
„ be thirsty	avoir soif	avwahr swahf
„ beat	battre	battr'
„ begin	commencer	commahnseh
„ believe	croire	crwahr
„ blame	blâmer	blah-meh
„ boil	bouillir	booyeer
„ borrow	emprunter	ahnprunteh
„ breakfast	déjeuner	deh-zhern-eh
„ bring	apporter	apporteh
„ build	bâtir	bah-teer
„ button ; un-	boutonner ; dé-	boo-ton-neh ; deh-
„ buy	acheter	ash-teh
„ carry	porter	por-teh
„ chat	causer	coh-zeh
„ compare	comparer	conparreh
„ consent	consentir	consahnteer
„ continue	continuer	contee-nēu-eh
„ cook	cuire	kēueer
„ cough	tousser	toosseh
„ cover	couvrir	coovreer

* See "French Grammar Self-Taught," pp. 56-96, and 104-120.

Italic s and e silent ; thick n indicates nasal ; apostrophe indicates suppressed vowel.

English.	French.	Pronunciation.
to dance	*danser*	dahn-seh
,, decide	*décider*	dehseedeh
,, deny	*nier*	nee-eh
,, depart, go away	*partir*	pahr-teer
,, descend	*descendre*	deh-sahn-dr'
,, desire, wish(for)	*désirer*	deh-zee-reh
,, dine	*dîner*	deeneh
,, do, make	*faire*	fair
,, doubt	*douter*	dooteh
,, draw, pull	*tirer*	teereh
— (a picture)	*dessiner*	des-see-neh
,, dream	*rêver*	raiveh
,, dress	*s'habiller*	sab-ee-yeh
,, drink	*boire*	bwahr
,, dwell, live	*demeurer*	dermērreh
,, eat	*manger*	mahn-zheh
,, exchange	*changer*	shahn-zheh
,, exclaim	*s'écrier*	seh-cree-eh
,, excuse	*excuser*	exkēuzeh
,, explain	*expliquer, déclarer*	expleekeh, deh-clahreh
,, fall	*tomber*	tonbeh
,, feel (in mind)	*sentir*	sahnteer
,, find	*trouver*	trooveh
,, finish	*finir*	feeneer
,, follow	*suivre*	sēueevr'
,, forget	*oublier*	ooblee-eh
,, get, obtain	*obtenir*	obterneer
,, get up	*se lever*	ser l'veh
,, give	*donner*	donneh
,, go	*aller*	alleh
,, go in	*entrer*	ahntreh
,, go out	*sortir*	sohr-teer
,, grow	*croître*	crwah-tr'
,, hate	*hair*	ah-eer
,, have	*avoir*	avwahr
,, hear	*entendre*	ahn-tahn-dr'
,, hesitate	*hésiter*	ehzeeteh
,, hide	*cacher*	cash-eh
,, hope	*espérer*	ess-peh-reh
,, imagine	*imaginer*	ee-mah-zhee-neh
,, intend	*se proposer*	ser pro-poh-zeh

Italic *r* and *t* silent; thick n indicates nasal; apostrophe indicates suppressed vowel.

G*

English.	French.	Pronunciation.
to introduce (one)	*présenter à*	preh-zahnteh ah
— (a thing)	*introduire*	antrodeüeer
„ jump	*sauter*	soh-teh
„ know	*savoir*	sav-wahr
— (a person)	*connaître*	con-naitr'
„ laugh	*rire*	reer
„ lay the table-	*mettre le couvert*	mettrer l' coovair
„ learn　[cloth	*apprendre*	apprahndr'
„ lend	*prêter*	praiteh
„ lie down	*se coucher*	ser coosheh
„ live (be alive)	*vivre*	veevr'
„ look for	*chercher*	shairsheh
„ lose	*perdre*	pairdr'
„ love	*aimer*	aimeh
„ marry (take in	*se marier avec*	ser marr'yeh av-ek
„ meet [marriage]	*rencontrer*	rahncontreh
„ mention	*mentionner*	mahn-s'yon-neh
„ object	*objecter*	ob-zhek-teh
„ obtain	*obtenir*	ob-ter-neer
„ offend	*offenser*	offahnseh
„ offer	*offrir*	offreer
„ open	*ouvrir*	oovreer
„ order, command	*ordonner*	ohrdonneh
„ pack up	*empaqueter*	ahnpahkteh
„ paint	*peindre*	pandr'
„ pay	*payer*	pai-yeh
„ plant	*planter*	plahnteh
„ play	*jouer*	zhweh
„ plough	*labourer*	lab-oor-eh
„ pluck, pick,	*cueillir*	kĕryeer
„ praise　[gather	*louer*	lweh
„ present	*présenter*	preh-zahnteh
„ prove	*prouver*	prooveh
„ put, put on	*mettre*	mettr'
„ read	*lire*	leer
„ reap	*moissonner*	mwahssonneh
„ receive	*recevoir*	rersservwahr
„ reckon, count	*compter*	conteh
„ refuse	*refuser*	rerfeüzeh
„ regret	*regretter*	rergretteh
„ remember	*se souvenir*	ser soov'neer

English.	French.	Pronunciation.
to repay	*rembourser*	rahnboorseh
,, repeat	*répéter*	reh-peh-teh
,, reply	*répliquer*	reh-pleekeh
,, rest [back]	*se reposer*	ser rerpozeh
,, return, come	*revenir*	rerv'neer
— (go back)	*retourner*	rertoorneh
— (give back)	*rendre*	rahndr'
,, ring the bell	*sonner*	sonneh
,, roast	*rôtir*	roh-teer
,, run	*courir*	cooreer
,, say, tell	*dire*	deer
,, search	*faire des re-*	fair dai rer-shairsh
,, see	*voir* [cherches]	vwahr
,, sell	*vendre*	vahndr'
,, serve	*servir*	sairveer
,, sew, stitch	*coudre*	coodr'
,, shave	*raser*	rahzeh
,, shine	*briller*	bree-yeh
,, show	*montrer*	montreh
,, sigh	*soupirer*	soopeereh
,, sign (letter, etc.)	*signer*	seenyeh
,, sit down	*s'asseoir*	sass-wahr
,, sleep	*dormir*	dohrmeer
,, sow (seed)	*semer*	sermeh
,, speak	*parler*	pahr-leh
,, spin	*filer*	feeleh
,, spoil	*gâter*	gahteh
,, steal	*voler*	voleh
,, study	*étudier*	eh-teud'yeh
,, swear	*jurer*	zheureh
,, take	*prendre*	prahndr'
,, take off, away	*ôter*	ohteh
,, take a walk	*faire une prome-*	fair eun prom-nahd
,, taste	*goûter* [nade]	gooteh
,, tell (a tale)	*raconter*	raconteh
,, thank	*remercier*	rermairs'yeh
,, think	*penser*	pahnseh
,, throw	*jeter*	zher-teh
,, touch	*toucher*	toosheh
,, translate	*traduire*	tradeueer
,, travel	*voyager*	vwah-yah-zheh

Italic *r* and *i* silent; thick **n** indicates nasal; apostrophe indicates suppressed vowel.

English.	French.	Pronunciation.
to unpack	*dépaqueter*	deh-pakteh
,, **want**	*avoir besoin de*	av-wahr berzwan der
,, **wash**	*laver*	lahveh
,, **weep**	*pleurer*	plērreh
,, **weigh**	*peser*	perzeh
,, **wish**	*souhaiter*	soo-aiteh
,, **wish, be willing**	*vouloir*	voolwahr
,, **work**	*travailler*	travahyeh
,, **wrap up**	*envelopper*	ahnv'loppeh
,, **write**	*écrire*	eh-creer

Adverbs, Conjunctions, & Prepositions*
Adverbes, conjonctions et prépositions

About	*environ*	ahnveeron
— (concerning)	*au sujet de*	oh seūzhai der
above	*dessus*	desseū
above all	*surtout*	seūrtoo
according to	*suivant*	seūeevahn
across	*à travers*	ah travair
after	*après*	aprai
afterwards	*ensuite, puis*	ahnseūeet, peūee
again	*encore*	ahncor
against (opposed to)	*contre*	contr'
all at once, sudden-	*tout à coup*	toot-ah-coo
almost [ly	*presque*	presk
alone, solely	*seul*	sērl
already	*déjà*	deh-zhah
also, too, besides	*aussi*	ohsee
although	*quoique*	kwah-ker
always	*toujours*	too-zhoor
amidst	*au milieu de*	oh meel-yēr der
among	*parmi*	pahr-mee
and	*et*	ai
anywhere	*n'importe où*	nanport oo
around, *adv.*	*autour, à l'entour*	ohtoor, ah lahntoor
as...as	*aussi...que*	ohsee...ker
as much (as) } as many (as) }	*autant (que)*	ohtahn (ker)
as soon (as)	*aussitôt (que)*	ohseetoh (ker)
at	*à*	ah
at first	*d'abord*	dab-or

* See "French Grammar Self-Taught," pp. 97-103.

English.	French.	Pronunciation.
at last	enfin	ahnfan
at least	au moins	oh mwan
at (the) most	au plus	oh pleū
at once	tout de suite	tood'seūeet
at present	en ce moment	ahns'-momahn
dably	mal	mal
beautifully	admirablement	admeerahblermahn
because	parce que	parss ker
before (time); —	avant; devant	avahn; dervahn
behind [(place)	derrière	dair-yair
below, adv.	en bas	ahn bah
below, beneath	dessous	dessoo
besides, beyond	outre	ootr'
better	mieux	m'yēr
between, among(st)	entre, parmi	ahntr', par-mee
briefly, in short	bref	bref
but	mais	mai
by, at	chez	shai
by turns	tour à tour	toor-ah-toor
calmly	tranquillement	trahnkeel'mahn
close to	près de	prai der
consequently	par conséquent	pahr conseh-kahn
daily	journellement	zhoornell'mahn
down, downwards	en bas	ahn bah
during	pendant	pahndahn
early, betimes	tôt	toh
either...or	ou...ou	oo...oo
elsewhere	ailleurs	ah-yērr
even if	quand même	kahn maim
everywhere	partout	pahr-too
exactly	exactement	exactermahn
exceedingly	excessivement	exsesseev-mahn
excellently	excellemment	exsellamahn
except, conj.	à moins de	ah mwan der
—, prep.	excepté, hormis	exsepteh, ormee
except that	excepté que	exsepteh ker
faithfully	fidèlement	feedailmahn
far from	loin de	lwan der
foolishly	follement	follmahn
for, conj.; —, prep.	pour; car	poor; cahr
formerly	autrefois	ohtrerfwah

English.	French.	Pronunciation.
from	*de*	de*r*
fully	*pleinement*	plain-mah**n**
further	*plus loin*	plēu lwa**n**
gladly, readily	*avec plaisir*	av-ek plai*z*ee*r*
hardly	*à peine*	ah pai*n*
here	*ici*	ee-see
herewith	*ci-inclus*	see-anclēu
honestly	*honnêtement*	onnaitmah**n**
honourably	*honorablement*	onohrahbler**mahn**
how?	*comment ?*	commah**n** ?
how (in exclama-	*comme, que*	comm, ke*r*
however [tions)	*cependant*	serpahndah**n**
how much?	*combien ?*	con-b'ya**n**
if	*si*	see
if not	*si non*	see no**n**
if only	*pourvu que*	poorvēu ke*r*
immediately	*tout de suite*	tood'sēueet
in, within	*dans, en*	dah**n**, ah**n**
in case	*en cas que*	ah**n** cah ke*r*
in future	*à l'avenir*	ah lahv'nee*r*
in spite of	*malgré*	malgreh
indeed	*vraiment*	vraimah**n**
inside	*dedans*	derdah**n**
instead of	*au lieu de*	oh l'yē*r* de*r*
kindly	*avec bienveillance*	av-ek b'yan-vai-[yah**n**ss
late	*tard*	tah*r*
less	*moins*	mwa**n**
like, as	*comme*	comm
little	*peu*	pēu
—— (but little)	*guère*	gai*r*
more	*plus*	plēu
more and more	*de plus en plus*	de*r* plēu*z* **ahn** plēu
much	*beaucoup*	bohcoo
near	*près*	prai
nearly	*presque*	presk
neither...nor	*ni...ni*	nee...**nee**
never	*jamais*	zham-a*i*
next to	*près de* [*ment*	prai de*r* [**mahn**
nicely	*bien, agréable-*	b'yan, agreh-ahbler-
not	*non, ne pas, ne point*	non, ne*r* pah, ne*r* pwan

English.	French.	Pronunciation.
not at all	*point du tout*	pwan dēu too
not yet	*pas encore*	pahz ̑ahncor
now	*maintenant*	man-t'nahn
nowhere	*nulle part*	nēul pahr
of	*de*	der
of course	*cela va sans dire*	s'la va sahn deer
often	*souvent*	soovahn
on, upon	*sur*	sēur
on account of	*à cause de*	ah cohz der
on the contrary	*au contraire*	oh contrair
on the left	*à gauche*	ah gohsh
on the opposite side	*au delà de*	oh d'lah der
on the right	*à droite*	ah drwaht
on this side	*de ce côté-ci*	der s'coh-teh-see
only	*seulement*	serlmahn
opposite (to)	*vis-à-vis (le)*	veez-ah-vee (der)
or	*ou*	oo
otherwise	*autrement*	ohtrermahn
out of	*hors de*	or der
outside	*dehors*	der-or
over	*sur*	sēur
perhaps	*peut-être*	per-taitr'
presently, soon	*tout à l'heure*	tootahlērr
previously	*auparavant*	ohpar-avahn
purposely	*exprès*	ex-prai
quickly	*vite*	veet
quite, altogether	*tout à fait*	toot-ah-fai
quietly	*en silence*	ahn seelahnss
rather, preferably	*plutôt*	plēutoh
—, somewhat	*assez*	asseh
readily, promptly	*promptement*	pront-mahn
round (a-), *prep.*	*autour de*	ohtoor der
scarcely	*à peine*	ah pain
seldom, rarely	*rarement*	rahr-mahn
since, *adv., prep.*	*depuis*	derpēuee
—, *conj.*	*puisque*	pēueesk'
so	*si*	see
so much, so many	*tant*	tahn
so much the better	*tant mieux*	tahn m'yēr
somehow	*d'une manière ou d'une autre*	dēun man-yair oo dēun ohtr'

English.	French.	Pronunciation.
sometimes	quelquefois	kelkerfwah
soon	bientôt	b'yan-toh
suddenly	subitement	seŭbeetmahn
that, conj.	que	ker
that is	c'est-à-dire	sait-ah-deer
then, adv.; —, conj.	alors ; donc	al-ohr ; don
thence	de là	der-lah
thenceforth	dès lors	dai lohr
there	là	lah
therefore	ainsi donc	ansee don
thoughtfully	avec prévenance	av-ek prehv-nahnss
through	par, à travers	pahr, ah trahvair
thus, so	ainsi	ansee
till, until	jusqu'à	zheŭskah
till now	jusqu'à présent	zheŭskah preh-zahn
to	à	ah
together	ensemble	ahnsahnbl'
too much, too	trop	troh
towards	vers	vair
under	sous	soo
undoubtedly	indubitablement	andeŭbeetahblermahn
unless	à moins que	ah mwan ker
up, upwards	en haut	ahn oh
upon	sur	seŭr
very	très, fort	trai, fohr
weekly, every week	toutes les se-	toot lai s'main
well	bien [maines	b'yan
when	lorsque, quand	lorsk, kahn
whence ?	d'où ?	doo ?
where ?	où ?	oo ?
whether, 1	que, si	ker, see
while	pendant	pahndahn
whilst	tandis que	tahndee ker
why ?	pourquoi ?	poorkwah ?
willingly	volontiers	volont'yeh
with	avec	av-ek
—, near	chez, auprès	shai, ohprai
within	dedans	derdahn
without	sans	sahn
yearly	annuellement	an-neŭel-mahn
yet, still	pourtant	poortahn

Italic s and t silent ; thick n indicates nasal ; apostrophe indicates suppressed vowel.

Tables of Adjectives, Pronouns, and the Auxiliary Verbs.

DEMONSTRATIVE ADJECTIVES.

	Masc. Sing.	Fem. Sing.	M. & F. Plural.
This, that,	*ce*, ser *cet*, set	*cette*, set.	These, those, *ces*, sai.

POSSESSIVE ADJECTIVES.

	Masc. Sing.	Fem. Sing.	M. & F. Plural.
My,	*mon*, mon	*ma*, mah	*mes*, mai
Thy,	*ton*, ton	*ta*, tah	*tes*, tai
His, her, its,	*son*, son	*sa*, sah	*ses*, sai
Our,	*notre*, notr'		*nos*, noh
Your,	*votre*, votr'		*vos*, voh
Their,	*leur*, lērr		*leur*, lērr.

INDEFINITE ADJECTIVES.

Any, no, none, *aucun, -e*, oh-kun, oh-kēun ; *nul, -le*, neūl	Same, self, *même*, maim
	Several, *plusieurs*, pleūzyērr
Other, *autre*, ohtr'	Whatever, *quelconque*, kelkonk
Some, someone, certain, *certain, -e*, sairtan, sairten	Some, a few, *quelque, quelques*, kelker
Each, every, *chaque*, shahk	Such, *tel, -le*, tel
Many a, *maint, -e*, man, mant	All, every, *tout, -e*, too, toot.

PERSONAL PRONOUNS.

Subject.	Conjunctive. Direct Object.	Indirect Object.	Disjunctive. Subj. or Obj.
I, *je*, zher	me, *me*, mer	to me, *me*, mer	*moi*, mwah
thou, *te*, ter	thee, *te*, ter	to thee, *te*, ter	*toi*, twah
he, *il*, eel	him, *le*, ler	to him, to her,	*lui*, leūee
she, *elle*, el	her, *la*, lah	*lui*, leūee	*elle*, el
we, *nous*, noo	us, *nous*, noo	to us, *nous*, noo	*nous*, noo
you, *vous*, voo	you, *vous*, voo	to you, *vous*, voo	*vous*, voo
they, m. *ils*, eel f. *elles*, el	them, *les*, lai	to them, *leur*, lērr	m. *eux*, ēr f. *elles*, el.

En, ahn, of it, of them ; *y*, ee, to it, to them (mostly of things).

DEMONSTRATIVE PRONOUNS.

	Masc. Sing.		
It, that, *ce*, ser. This, *ceci*, sersee. That, *cela*, serlah; *ça*, sah

	Masc. Sing.	Fem. Sing.	Masc. Plural.	Fem. Plur.
That, those,	*celui*, serleūee	*celle*, sel	*ceux*, sēr	*celles*, sel
This, these,	*celui-ci*, serleūee-see	*celle-ci*, sel-see	*ceux-ci*, sēr-see	*celles-ci*, sel-see
That, those,	*celui-là*, serleūee-lah	*celle-là*, sel-lah	*ceux-là*, sēr-lah	*celles-là*, sel-lah.

POSSESSIVE PRONOUNS.

	Masc. Sing.	Fem. Sing.	Masc. Plural.	Fem. Plural.
Mine,	*le mien,* ler m'yan	*la mienne,* lah m'yen	*les miens,* lai m'yan	*les miennes,* lai m'yen
Thine,	*le tien,* ler t'yan	*la tienne,* lah t'yen	*les tiens,* lai t'yan	*les tiennes,* lai t'yen
His, hers, its,	*le sien,* ler s'yan	*la sienne,* lah s'yen	*les siens,* lai s'yan	*les siennes,* lai s'yen
Ours,	*le (la) nôtre,* ler (lah) notr'		*les nôtres,* lai notr'	
Yours,	*le (la) vôtre,* ler (lah) votr'		*les vôtres,* lai votr'	
Theirs,	*le (la) leur,* ler (lah) lērr		*les leurs,* lai lērr.	

(Plural)

RELATIVE PRONOUNS.

Of Persons.	Of Things.
Who, *qui,* kee	Which, *qui,* kee
Whose, *dont,* don ; *de qui,* der kee	Whose, *dont,* don
Whom, *que,* ker	Which, *que,* ker.

Who, which,	*lequel,* lerkel	*lesquels,* laikel	*laquelle,* lahkel	*lesquelles,* laikel
Whose, of which,	*duquel,* dēukel	*desquels,* daikel	*de laquelle,* der lahkel	*desquelles* daikel
To whom, to which,	*auxquel,* ohkel	*auxquels,* ohkel	*à laquelle,* ah lahkel	*auxquelles,* ohkel
Whom, which,	*lequel,* lerkel	*lesquels,* laikel	*laquelle,* lahkel	*lesquelles,* laikel.

INTERROGATIVE PRONOUNS.

Of Persons.	Of Things.
Who? *qui? qui est-ce qui?* kee? kee ess kee?	What? *que? qu'est-ce qui?* ker? kess kee ?
Whose? *de qui?* der kee?	Of what? *de quoi?* der kwah?
To whom? *à qui?* ah kee?	To what? *à quoi?* ah kwah?
Whom? *qui? qui est-ce que?* kee? kee ess ker?	What? *que? qu'est-ce que?* ker? kess ker?

INDEFINITE PRONOUNS.

Both, *l'un et l'autre,* lern ai lohtr' [oo lohtr'	None, *aucun-e,* ohkun, ohkēun
	Everything, all, *tout,* too
Either, *l'un ou l'autre,* lern	Nothing, *rien ne,* r'yan ner
Neither, *ni l'un ni l'autre,* nee lun nee lohtr' [lohtr'	Someone, *quelqu'un -e,* kel- kun, kelkēun
One another, *l'un l'autre,* lun	No one, nobody, *nul,* nēul
Each one, everyone, *chacun-e,* shahkun, shahkēun	Others, *autrui, d'autres, d'au- cuns,* ohtrēuee, dohtr', dohkun
Some, *quelques-uns -unes,* kelkerz-un, kelkerz-ēun	Several, *plusieurs,* plēuzyērr
	Whoever, *quiconque.* keeconk

THE AUXILIARY VERBS.*

To Have, *Avoir*.

Infinitive—Present.

To have, *avoir*, avwahr

Infinitive—Past.

To have had, *avoir eu*, avwahr eū

Present—Participle.

Having, *ayant*, ayahn

Past—Participle.

Had, *eu*, eū.

Indicative—Present.

I have, &c., *j'ai*, zhai	*nous avons*, nooz avon
tu as, teū ah	*vous avez*, vooz avai
il, elle a, eel, el ah	*ils, elles ont*, eel, el zon

Imperfect.

I had *or* was having, &c.

j'avais, zhavai	*nous avions*, nooz avvyon
tu avais, teū avai	*vous aviez*, vooz avvyeh
il, elle avait, eel, el avai	*ils, elles avaient*, eel, el zavai

Past Definite.

I had, &c., *j'eus*, zheū..	*nous eûmes*, nooz eūm
tu eus, teū eū	*vous eûtes*, vooz eūt
il, elle eut, eel, el eū	*ils, elles eurent*, eel, el zeūr

Future.

I shall have, &c.,	
j'aurai, zhohrai	*nous aurons*, nooz ohron
tu auras, teū ohrah	*vous aurez*, vooz ohreh
il, elle aura, eel, el ohrah	*ils, elles auront*, eel, el zohron

Conditional—Present.

I should *or* would have, &c.

j'aurais, zhohrai	*nous aurions*, nooz ohryon
tu aurais, teū ohrai	*vous auriez*, vooz ohryai
il, elle aurait, eel, el ohrai	*ils, elles auraient*, eel, el zohrai

Imperative.

Have (thou), *aie*, ai	let us have, *ayons*, ayon
	have (ye), *ayez*, ayeh

Subjunctive—Present.

That I may have, that I have,

que j'aie (ker zhai) [&c.
que tu aies (ai)
qu'il, qu'elle ait (ai)
que nous ayons (ayon)
que vous ayez (ayeh)
qu'ils, qu'elles aient (ai)

Subjunctive—Imperfect.

That I might have, &c.

que j'eusse (ker zheūss)
que tu eusses (eūss)
qu'il, qu'elle eût (eū)
que nous eussions (eūssyon)
que vous eussiez (eūssyeh)
qu'ils, qu'elles eussent (eūss)

* For the conjugation and grammar of the verbs—auxiliary, regular and irregular—see Marlborough's "French Grammar Self-Taught," pp. 56-96 and 104-120.

To Be, *Être.*

<table>
<tr><td>

Infinitive—Present.

To be, *être*, aitr'

</td><td>

Infinitive—Past.

To have been, *avoir été*, avvahr ehteh

</td></tr>
<tr><td>

Present Participle.

Being, *étant*, ehtahn

</td><td>

Past Participle.

Been, *été*, ehteh

</td></tr>
</table>

Indicative—Present.

I am, &c.,	*je suis*, zher sẽuee	*nous sommes*, noo som
	tu es, tẽu ai	*vous êtes*, vooz ait
	il, elle est, eel, el ai	*ils, elles sont*, eel, el son

Imperfect.

I was, &c.,	*j'étais*, zhehtai	*nous étions*, nooz ehtyon
	tu étais, tẽu ehtai	*vous étiez*, vooz ehtyeh
	il, elle était, eel, el ehtai	*ils, elles étaient*, eel, el zehtai

Past Definite.

I was, &c.,	*je fus*, zher fẽu	*nous fûmes*, noo fẽum
	tu fus, tẽu fẽu	*vous fûtes*, voo fẽut
	il, elle fut, eel, el fẽu	*ils, elles furent*, eel, el fẽur

Future.

I shall be, &c.

je serai, zher s'rai	*nous serons*, noo s'ron
tu seras, tẽu s'rah	*vous serez*, voo s'reh
il, elle sera, eel, el s'rah	*ils, elles seront*, eel, el s'ron

Conditional—Present.

I should be, &c.

je serais, zher s'rai	*nous serions*, noo seryon
tu serais, tẽu s'rai	*vous seriez*, voo seryeh
il, elle serait, eel, el s'rai	*ils, elles seraient*, eel, el s'rai

Imperative.

| Be (thou), *sois*, swah | let us be, *soyons*, swahyon |
| | be (ye), *soyez*, swahyeh |

<table>
<tr><td>

Subjunctive—Present.

That I may be, that I be, &c.

  que je sois (kerzh' swah)
  que tu sois (swah)
  qu'il, qu'elle soit (swah)
  que nous soyons (swahyon)
  que vous soyez (swahyeh)
  qu'ils, qu'elles soient (swah)

</td><td>

Subjunctive—Imperfect.

That I might be, &c.

  que je fusse (kerzh' fẽuss)
  que tu fusses (fẽuss)
  qu'il, qu'elle fût (fẽu)
  que nous fussions (fẽussyon)
  que vous fussiez (fẽussyeh)
  qu'ils, qu'elles fussent (fẽuss)

</td></tr>
</table>

CONVERSATIONAL PHRASES & SENTENCES*

Greetings and Polite Expressions
Saluts et politesses

NOTE.—In France it is usual to preface any inquiry with *"Pardon, monsieur"* (pardon me, sir), raising the hat. So, too, *"s'il vous plait"* (if you please) may be added to requests, enquiries, etc., as politeness is always appreciated in France.

When speaking to persons about their relations (not one's own) use *Monsieur, Madame, Mademoiselle* as a mark of respect, *e.g.* :—

Madame votre mère est-elle revenue ?
(Has your mother returned ?)

Monsieur votre père est allé à la campagne.
(Your father has gone into the country.)

In making use of the above forms, care must be taken not to use them inappropriately ; in the case of servants or children it is better to avoid them altogether than to use them out of place.

The French never address their relatives as " Uncle," " Aunt," etc., but say *" Mon oncle," "ma tante,"* etc.

The expressions, *the, this,* or *that lady,* or *gentleman,* are usually rendered in French by *Madame* or *Monsieur* alone; as, *Madame a apporté de la musique* (the lady has brought some music).

English.	French.	Pronunciation.
Good morning (afternoon), Mr. A.	*Bonjour, Monsieur A.*	bon-zhoor, mers'yerr A.
Good day, sir	*Bonjour, monsieur*	bon-zhoor, mers'yer
Good night, miss [Mrs. A.	*Bonsoir, madmoiselle [A.*	bonswahr, mad'mwahzell [A.
Good evening,	*Bonsoir, Madame*	bon-swahr, mad-ahm
Good-bye, farewell	*Adieu*	ad-yēr'
— (for the present)	*Au revoir*	oh rer-vwahr
How do you do?} How are you ? }	*Comment allez-vous?*	commahnt alleh-voo ?
Are you quite well ? [you	*Vous allez bien ?* [merci	vooz alleh b'yan ? [mairsee
Quite well, thank How is Mr. F. ?	*Je vais très bien, Comment se porte Monsieur F. ?*	zher vai trai b'yan, commahn ser pohrt mers'yer F. ?

Italic *v* and *i* silent ; thick n indicates nasal ; apostrophe indicates suppressed vowel.
*See " French Equivalents," p. 15.

(96)

English.	French.	Pronunciation.
I am so pleased to meet you	*Je suis charmé de vous rencontrer*	zher swee shahr'meh der voo rahn-con.eh
The pleasure is mine	*C'est moi qui en suis charmé*	sai mwah kee ahn seūee shahr'meh
I hope we may meet again	*Au plaisir de vous revoir !*	oh plai-zeer der voo rervwahr !
Pleased to make your acquaintance	*Charmé(e) de faire votre connaissance*	shahr'meh der fair votrer connaissahnss'
This is a pleasure!	*Quel plaisir !*	kell plai-zeer !
I must go now [again	*Il me faut partir maintenant*	eel mer foh pahr'teer mant'nahn
I hope to come	*J'espère revenir*	zhespair rerv'neer
Will you excuse me ?	*Excusez-moi, je vous prie*	exkeūz-eh-mwah, zher voo pree
Must you go yet ?	*Faut-il que vous partiez déjà ?*	fohteel ker voo pahrt'-yeh deh-zhah ?
I'm afraid I can't stay any longer	*Je crains de ne pouvoir rester plus*	zher cran der n' poovwahr resteh pleū
Thank you; thanks	*Merci* [longtemps	mairsee [longtahn
No, thanks	*Non, merci*	non, mairsee
Please (If you —)	*S'il vous plaît*	seel voo plai
I thank you	*Je vous remercie*	zher voo rermairsee
Many thanks	*Mille remercie-*	meel rermairseemahn
Much obliged	*Bien obligé* [ments	b'yan oblee-zheh
I am very much obliged to you	*Je vous suis infiniment obligé*	zher voo sweez an-fee-neemahn oblee-zheh
Excuse (pardon) me, sir	*Excusez-moi, monsieur* [pardon	exkeūzeh-mwah, mers'yer [pahr'don
I beg (your) pardon	*Pardonnez-moi ;*	pahr'donneh-mwah ;
I'm sorry, miss	*Je suis fâché, mademoiselle*	zher seūee fah-sheh, mad'mwah-zell [sheh
I am so sorry	*J'en suis si fâché*	zhahn seūee see fah-sheh
I am very sorry	*— — bien fâché*	zhahn seūee b'yan fah-sheh
It is nothing	*Ce n'est rien*	s'nai r'yan [sheh
There is no harm done [it	*Il n'y a pas de mal*	eel n'yah pah d' mal
Pray don't mention	*Il n'y a pas de quoi*	eel n'yah pah d' kwah
I must apologise	*Je vous fais mille excuses*	zher voo fai meel exkeūz

* At table *merci* may be used as the equivalent of "No, thank you."

English.	French.	Pronunciation.
It doesn't matter	N'importe [cuses	nan-port
Make my apologies	Faites mes ex-	fait maiz͡ exkeūz
Permit me to apologise [needed]	Permettez-moi de faire mes excuses	pairmetteh-mwah der fair maiz͡ exkeūz
No apology is	Ne faites pas	ner fait pah dexkeūz
Don't apologise	d'excuses	
It was my fault	C'était ma faute	seh-tai ma foht
Can I be of any assistance to you?	Puis je vous être utile? [mable	peūee-zh'vooz͡ ai-tr'eū teel? [bl'
You are very kind	Vous êtes bien ai-	vooz͡ ait b'yan͡ aimah-
Not at all	Pas du tout	pah deū too [deh?
May I ask?	Puis-je demander?	peūee-zh' dermahn-
Have the kindness (goodness)	Voulez-vous avoir la bonté?	vooleh-vooz avwahr la bonteh?
Allow me	Permettez-moi	pairmetteh-mwah
With pleasure	Avec plaisir	av-ek plaizeer
Yes, sir	Oui, monsieur	wee, mers'yer
No, madam	Non, madame	non, mad-ahm

Useful and Necessary Expressions
Expressions utiles et nécessaires

Bring me	Apportez-moi	appohrteh-mwah
Send me	Envoyez-moi	ahn-vwah-yeh-mwah
Tell me	Dites-moi [dire?	deet-mwah
Will you tell me?	Voulez-vous me	vooleh-voo mer deer?
Do you speak English, French?	Parlez-vous anglais, français?	pahrleh-vooz͡ ahnglai, frahnsai?
I do not speak French	Je ne parle pas français	zhern' pahrl pah frahnsai
Is there anyone here who speaks English?	Y a-t-il ici quelqu'un qui parle anglais?	yaht-eel eesee kelkun kee pahrl ahnglai?
Please speak more slowly [little	Parlez plus lentement, s'il vous plaît [peu	pahrleh pleū lahnt'-mahn, seel voo plai [per
I speak English a	Je parle anglais un	zher pahrl ahnglai un
Can you read French?	Pouvez-vous lire le français? [bien	pooveh-voo leer ler frahnsai?
You read very well	Vous lisez très	voo leezeh trai-b'yan
How long have learnt?	Depuis quand l'apprenez-vous?	derpeūee kahn lapprerneh-voo?

English.	French.	Pronunciation.
A short time only	Depuis peu de temps [seigné?	derpẽuee pẽr der tahn [yeh ?
Who taught you?	Qui vous a en-	kee vooz ah ahnsayn-
I do not find the pronunciation very difficult	Je ne le trouve pas très difficile à prononcer	zhern' ler troov pah trai dee-fee-seel ah pronon-seh
You have a good accent	Vous avez bon accent [avez dit?	vooz avveh bon ak-sahn [dee?
What did you say?	Qu'est-ce que vous	kess ker vooz avveh
I have nothing to say against it	Je n'ai rien à y dire [mandé?	zh' nai r'yan ah ee deer [deh ?
What did you ask?	Qu'avez-vous de-	kavveh-voo d'mahn-
Speak louder [fy?	Parlez plus haut	pahrleh plẽu hoh
What does it signi-	Qu'importe ?	kan-pohrt ?
It is all the same	Cela m'est égal	s'la mait ehgal
Never mind [to me	N'importe	nan-port
What is the matter?	Qu'y a-t-il ?	kee-ahteel ?
Nothing	Il n'y a rien	eel nee-ah r'yan
What is it about?	De quoi s'agit-il ?	der kwah sah-zheet-eel?
It is all a mistake	C'est entièrement une erreur	sait ahnt'yair-mahn ẽun airrẽrr
What is to be done?	Que faire ?	ker fair ?
I haven't a notion	Je n'en ai pas l'idée	zh' nahneh pah leedeh'
That depends	C'est selon	sai s'lon
Do you understand	Comprenez-vous ?	conprerneh-voo ?
I understand	Je comprends	zh' conprahn
I don't understand you	Je ne vous com- prends pas	zhern' voo conprahn pah
Take this	Prenez ceci	prerneh ser-see
Take this away	Emportez ceci	ahnpohrteh ser-see
Make haste !	Dépêchez-vous !	deh-paisheh-voo !
Come along	Venez donc	verneh don
Take care !	Prenez garde !	prerneh gahr'd !
Look out !	Faites attention !	faitz attahn-s'yon !
Listen !	Ecoutez !	eh-cooteh !
Come in! Walk in!	Entrez ! [ici]	ahntreh ! [eesee !
(Come) here !	Approchez! Venez	approsheh ! vernehz
Go away !	Allez-vous en !	alleh-vooz ahn !
This way; that way	Par ici ; par là	pahr' eesee ; pahr' lah
Too soon ; too late	Trop tôt; trop tard	troh toh ; troh tahr
Very well	Très bien	trai-b'yan

English.	French.	Pronunciation.
Not very well	*Pas très bien*	pah trai-b'yan
What do you want?	*Que voulez-vous ?*	ker vooleh-voo ?
Of course	*Cela va sans dire*	s'lah vah sahn deer
On the contrary	*Au contraire*	oh contrair'
Once for all	*Une fois pour*	ēun fwah poor toot
Between ourselves	*Entre nous* [*toutes*	ahntrer noo
After all	*Au bout du compte*	oh boo dēu cont
The other day	*L'autre jour*	loh-trer-zhoor
At the end of a year	*Au bout d'un an*	oh boo dērn ahn
Everybody knows it [sequence	*Tout le monde le sait*	tool' mond ler sai
That is of no con-	*Cela n'est rien*	s'la nai r'yan
I remember it	*Je m'en souviens*	zher mahn soov'yan
Without a doubt; beyond question	*Hors de doute*	or der doot
No great thing	*Pas grand' chose*	pah grahn shohz
Ever so little	*Tant soit peu*	tahn swah pēr
Sooner or later	*Tôt ou tard* [*quille*	toht-oo-tahr' [keel
Leave me alone	*Laissez-moi tran-*	laisseh-mwah trahn-
You are joking	*Vous plaisantez*	voo plaizahnteh
You are right	*Vous avez raison*	vooz avveh raizon
I give it up	*J'y renonce*	zhee rer-nonss
So much the more	*D'autant plus*	dohtahn plēu
For want of time	*Faute de temps*	foht der tahn
With all my heart	*De tout mon cœur*	der too mon kērr
Do your best [where ?	*Faites de votre mieux* [*que part?*	fait der votrer m'yēr
Are you going any-	*Allez-vous quel-*	alleh-voo kelker pahr' ?
I am going to town	*Je vais à la ville*	zher vaiz ah la veel
From top to bottom	*De fond en comble*	der font-ahn conbl'
Upstairs	*En haut*	ahn hoh
Downstairs	*En bas*	ahn bah [seh
I am in a hurry	*Je suis bien pressé*	zher sēuee b'yan pres-
Where have you come from ? [*pas*	*D'où venez-vous ?*	doo v'neh-voo ?
Don't go away	*Ne vous en allez*	nervooz ahn alleh pah
Don't stir	*Ne bougez pas*	ner boo-zheh pah
I shall go home	*J'irai à la maison*	zheerai ah la maizon
On horseback	*À cheval*	ah sh'val
He has come back	*Il est de retour*	eel ai der r'toor
Nor I either	*Ni moi non plus*	nee mwah non plēu

Italic *r* and *é* silent; thick **n** indicates nasal; apostrophe indicates suppressed vowel.

H*

English.	French.	Pronunciation.
In some way or other	D'une façon ou d'une autre [êtes	deūn fasson oo deūn oh-tr' [ait
That is just like you	Voilà comme vous	vwah-la comm vooz
Give him that from me [mine	Donnez-lui cela de ma part	donneh-leūee s'la d'ma pahr'
He is a friend of	Il est de mes amis	eel ai d' maiz ahmee
In the meantime	En attendant	ahn attahndahn
Will you kindly ?	Voulez-vous bien?	vooleh-voo b'yan ?
First of all	D'abord	dab-ohr
That is what vexes me [in	C'est ce qui me fâche	sess kee m' fahsh
He has just come	Il vient de rentrer	eel v'yan d' rahntreh
He pretends	Il fait semblant	eel fai sahnblahn
Don't imagine	N'allez pas croire	nalleh pah crwahr
Within every-body's reach	À la portée de tout le monde	ah-la porteh' der tool' mond
What good is it ?	À quoi bon ?	ah kwah bon ?
As for me	Quant à moi	kahnt ah mwah
In a good temper	De bonne humeur	der bun eūmērr
Unknown to me	À mon insu	ah mon an-seū
At the latest	Au plus tard	oh pleū tahr'
Where was I ?	Où en étais-je ?	oo ahn eh-taizh' ?
You speak at random	Vous parlez à tort et à travers	voo pahr'lehz ah tor ai ah travair
I did it in a hurry	Je l'ai fait à la hâte	zher lai fait ah la haht
He may say what he likes	Qu'il dise ce qu'il voudra	keel deez ser keel voodrah
He began to laugh	Il se mit à rire	eel ser meet ah reer
I cannot see any longer [for me	Je n'y vois plus [trois	zher nee vwah pleū [trwah
Three are enough	J'en ai assez de	zhahn ai asseh der
It only depends up-on you [the other	Il ne tient qu'à vous	eel ner t'yan kah voo
One is as good as	L'un vaut l'autre	lun voh lohtr'
I can do without it	Je m'en passerai	zher mahn pahss'rai
Will you give me — ?	Voulez-vous me donner — ?	vooleh-voo mer don-neh — ?
Everything con-sidered [same	À tout prendre	ah too prahndr'
He will do just the	Il en fera autant	eel ahn f'rah ohtahn
That is too much	C'en est trop	sahn ai troh

Italic r and t silent; thick n indicates nasal: apostrophe indicates suppressed vowel.

English.	French.	Pronunciation.
I am sure of what I say [you	Je suis sûr de mon fait	zher swee sēur der mon fait
I have come to tell	Je viens vous dire	zher v'yan voo deer
I have been told	On m'a dit	on mah dee
I don't think much of it	Je n'en fais pas grand cas	zher nahn fai pah grahn cah
No sooner said than done	Aussitôt dit, aussitôt fait	ohseetoh dee, ohseetoh fai
I can bear it no longer	Je ne peux plus le supporter	zhern' pēr pleū ler sēuppohrteh
I like being here	Je me plais ici	zher m' plaiz ee-see
As much as I can	Autant qu'il est en moi	ohtahn keel ait ahn mwah
That comes to the same thing	Cela revient au même [faute	s'la rerv'yant oh maim
It is not my fault	Ce n'est pas ma	ser nai pah ma foht
I value it very much	J'y tiens beaucoup	zhee t'yan bohcoo
I am used to it	J'y suis fait	zhee sēuee fai
I am not able to do it	Je ne suis pas à même de le faire	zhern' sēuee pahz ah maim der l' fair
Who is it calls me?	Qui est-ce qui m'appelle?	kee ess kee mappell?

Émotions Expressions of Emotion

English.	French.	Pronunciation.
What?	Comment? [nez	commahn?
You surprise me	Vous me surpre-	voo mer sēurprerneh
Is it possible?	Est-il possible?	ait-eel posseebl'?
Indeed!	En vérité! [ble	ahn veh-ree-teh!
That is impossible	Cela est impossi-	s'la ait anposseebl'
That cannot be	Cela ne se peut pas	s'la ner s' pēr pah
My fault	C'est ma faute	sai mah foht
Oh! it's nothing	Oh! ce n'est rien	oh! s'nai r'yan
I am sorry for it	J'en suis fâché	zhahn sēuee fah-sheh
What a pity!	Quel dommage!	kel dommahzh!
It is a sad thing	C'est bien fâcheux	sai b'yan fah-shēr
I am very glad	Je suis bien aise	zher sēuee b'yan aiz
It gives me much pleasure	Je m'en réjouis	zher mahn reh-zhwee
What a shame!	Quelle honte!	kell hont!
How could you do so?	Comment avez-vous pu faire cela	commahnt avveh-voo pēu fair s'la?

Italic r and s silent; thick n indicates nasal; apostrophe indicates suppressed vowel.

English.	French.	Pronunciation.
You are very much to blame [you	Vous êtes bien à blâmer [honte	vooz ait b'yan ah blah-meh
I am ashamed of	Vous me faites	voo mer fait hont
For shame!	Fi donc! [pas	fee donk!
Don't be angry	Ne vous fâchez	ner voo fah-sheh pah
Don't mention it	N'en parlez pas	nahn pahr'leh pah
I am quite vexed about it	J'en suis bien ennuyé [yeux!	zhahn sẽuee b'yan ahn-nẽuee-yeh
How vexing!	Que c'est ennu-	ker sait ahn-nwee-yẽr!
How beautiful!	Que c'est beau!	ker sai boh!
Help!	Au secours!	oh s'coor!

Making Enquiries   Questions

English.	French.	Pronunciation.
Where can I buy an English newspa-	Où peut-on ache- ter un journal an-	oo pẽuton ashteh un zhoornal ahnglai?
Where is...? [per?	Où est...? [glais?	oo ai...?
Which is the way to...?	Comment allez- vous à...?	commahnt alleh- vooz ah...?
How can I get to...? [ance?	Comment puis-je aller à...? [ture?	commahn pweezh- alleh ah...?
Is there a convey-	Y a-t-il une voi-	yahteel ẽun vwahtẽur?
Do you hear me?	M'entendez-vous?	mahntahndeh-voo?
Would you kindly...?	Voudriez-vous bien...?	vood-ree-eh-voo b'yan?
Do you understand me?	Me comprenez- vous?	mer conprerneh-voo?
What is that?	Qu'est-ce que cela?	kess ker s'la?
Do you know Mr. —?	Connaissez-vous Monsieur —?	connaisseh-voo mers'- yer —?
What do you call that?	Comment appelez- vous cela?	commahnt appleh-voo s'la?
What do you mean?	Que voulez-vous dire?	ker vooleh-voo deer?
What does that mean?	Qu'est-ce que cela veut dire? [il?	kess ker s'la vẽr deer?
What is that for?	À quoi cela sert-	ah kwah s'la sairt-eel?
Are you sure?	Êtes-vous sûr?	ait-voo sẽur?
Who is that?	Qui est ce mon- sieur, cette dame?	kee ai ser mers-yer, sett dahm?
Who is there?	Qui est là?	kee ai lah?
Is that Mr. —?	Est-ce M. —?	ess mers-yer —?

The Time

English	French	Pronunciation
What time is it?	*Quelle heure est-il*	kell ērr ait-eel?
Tell me the time	*Dites-moi quelle heure il est*	deet-mwah kell ērr eel ai
Is it late?	*Est-il tard?*	ait-eel tahr'?
It is still early	*Il est encore de bonne heure*	eel ait^ahncohr der bun^ērr
It is two o'clock	*Il est deux heures*	eel ai dērz^ērr
It will soon strike six	*Six heures vont sonner*	seez^ērr von sonneh
It has just struck five	*Cinq heures viennent de sonner*	sank^ērr v'yenn der sonneh
It's time to get up	*Il est temps de se lever*	eel ai tahn der s'lerveh
It is day	*Il fait jour*	eel fai zhoor
It is not late	*Il n'est pas tard*	eel nai pah tahr'
It is five minutes past seven	*Il est sept heures cinq (minutes)*	eel ai sett ērr sank (meeneŭt)
It's a quarter past one	*Il est une heure et quart*	eel ait^eŭn^ērr ai kahr'
Exactly five o'clock	*Cinq heures juste*	sank ērr zheŭst
Between four and five o'clock	*Entre quatre et cinq heures*	ahntrer kahtr' ai sank ērr
It is twenty (minutes) past two	*Il est deux heures vingt (minutes)*	eel ai dērz^ērr van (meeneŭt)
It is half-past six	*Il est six heures et demie*	eel ai seez^ērr ai d'mee
Is it already so late?	*Est-il déjà si tard?*	ait-eel deh-zhah see tahr'?
It is later than I thought	*Il est plus tard que je ne pensais*	eel ai pleŭ tahr' ker zher n' pahnsai
At a quarter to eight	*À huit heures moins un quart*	ah eŭeet ērr mwanz^un kahr'
It is time for breakfast	*Il est temps de déjeuner*	eel est tahn der deh-zherneh
It will soon be nine o'clock	*Il sera bientôt neuf heures*	eel serah b'yantoh nērv^ērr
It has just struck nine	*Neuf heures viennent de sonner*	nērv^ērr v'yenn der sonneh
It is not two yet	*Il n'est pas encore deux heures*	eel nai pahz^ahncor dērz^ērr

Italic *r* and *i* silent; thick **n** indicates nasal; apostrophe indicates suppressed vowel.

English	French	Pronunciation
It is just twelve (mid-day)	*Il est juste midi*	eel a*i* zhe͡ust meedee
Has it struck eleven yet?	*Est-ce que onze heures ont déjà sonné?*	ess ke*r* o**n**z ērr o**n** deh-zhah sonneh?
It is only ten	*Il n'est que dix heures*	eel na*i* ke*r* deez͡ērr
Twenty minutes to six	*Six heures moins vingt*	seez͡ērr mwa**n** va**n** [neu͡ee
It is nearly midnight	*Il est bientôt minuit*	eel a*i* b'ya**n**toh mee-
At what time?	*À quelle heure?*	ah kell ērr?
At seven-fifteen p.m.	*À sept heures quinze du soir*	ah set͡ērr ka**n**z de͡u swahr
By your watch?	*À votre montre?*	ah votre*r* mo**n**tr'?
My watch has stopped	*Ma montre s'est arrêtée*	ma mo**n**tr' sa*i*t arra*i*teh'
I have forgotten to wind it up	*J'ai oublié de la remonter*	zhai ooblee-eh de*r* la re*r*mo**n**teh

On Train

Will you please show your tickets?	*Montrez vos billets s'il vous plaît.*	mo**n**treh voh bee'ya*i* seel voo pla*i*
Am sorry but your ticket has expired and I am obliged to collect the regular fare and give you a receipt for same so that you can call on the Agent on arrival, and he will arrange refund if you are entitled to same.	*Je le regrette, mais votre billet n'est plus valable-je suis obligé de percevoir le prix d'un billet régulier. Je vais vous donner un reçu et vous pourrez aller voir l'Agent a votre arrivée pour vous faire rembourser, s'il y a lieu.*	zher le*r* r'grett ma*i* votr' bee'ya*i* na*i* ple͡u va-lahbl-zher se͡uee͡z obleezheh de*r* pa*i*rs'-vwar le*r* pree da**n** bee'ya*i* rehge͡ul-ueh. zher va*i* voo dunneh un re*r*se͡u a*i* voo poor-rehz͡alleh vwar la-zhah**n** ah votr' ahrree-veh poor voo fa*i*r rah**n**-boorseh, seel yah ly'ēr
How much is it?	*C'est combien?*	sa*i* co**n**b'ya**n**?
. . . dollars . . . cents, please	*. . . dollars . . . sous, s'il vous plaît*	. . . dollahr . . . soo, seel voo pla*i*
How old is this child, please?	*Quel est l'âge de cet enfant?*	kel a*i* lahzh de*r* set͡ahn-fah**n**
. . . years	*. . . ans*	. . . ah**n**

Italic *r* and *i* silent; thick **n** indicates nasal; apostrophe indicates suppressed vowel.

English	French	Pronunciation
According to my instructions	D'après mes instructions	dahprai maiẑˆanstreūks' yon
he should pay half fare	il doit payer un demi-billet	eel dwah paiʹyeh un dermee beeʹyai
he should pay full fare	il doit payer plein prix	eel dwah paiʹyeh plan pree

Trains, Tickets, Rates, etc. Passenger Inquiry

At what time do trains leave for?	A quelles heures portent les trains pour	ah kelẑˆērr pahrt lai tran poor
At nine a.m.	À neuf heures du matin	ah nervˆ-err deū matan
Madam, Miss or Sir: Daily	Tous les jours, madame, mlle. ou monsieur	too lai zhoor, madahm, mad'mwahzell, oo mers'yer
Daily except Sunday	Tous les jours excepté le dimanche	too lai zhoor exsepteh ler deemahnsh
Daily except Saturday and Sunday	Tous les jours excepté le samedi et le dimanche	too lai zhoor exsepteh ler sahmdee eh ler deemahnsh
Sunday, Monday, Tuesday, Wednesday, Thursday, Friday, Saturday	Dimanche, lundi, mardi, mercredi, jeudi, vendredi, samedi	deemahnsh, lundee, mardee, maircrerdee, zhērdee, vahndrerdee, sahmdee
At what time is the train due at destination?	A quelle heure le train arrive-t-il à destination?	ah kel ērr ler tran arreevt-ee'l ah daisteenasy'on
At . . .	A . . .	ah . . .
Any change of trains en route?	Faut-il changer de trains en route?	foht-eel shahnzheh der tran ahn root?
Yes, at . . .	Oui, à . . .	wee, ah . . .
No—no change	Non—aucun changement	non,—ohcun shahnzh'mahn
What is the fare to . . . ?	Quel est le prix d'un billet pour . . . ?	kel ai ler pree dun beeʹyai poor . . .
Single—first class	Première classe — simple	prermyair clahss-sanpl'
Round-trip—first class	Première classe — aller et retour	prermyair clahss—alleh eh rertoor

Italic r and i silent; thick n indicates nasal; apostrophe indicates suppressed vowel.

English	French	Pronunciation
Single—coach class	*Voiture ordinaire — simple*	vwahtêur ohrdeena*r — sa**n**pl'
Round-trip — coach class	*Voiture ordinaire — aller et retour*	vwahtêur ohrdeena*r — alleh eh re*rtour
Week-end	*Fin de semaine*	fa**n** de*r* se*r*mai**n**
Excursion	*Excursion*	exkêursyo**n**
For nuns	*Pour religieuses*	poor re*r*leezhyē*r*z
For a priest holding Canadian Passenger Association Certificate [ler	*Pour un prêtre muni d'un certificat de la Canadian Passenger Association*	poor e*r*n prai*t*r' mêuni du**n** sai*r*teefeecah de*r* lah Canadian Passenger Association
Commercial travel-	*Commis-voyageur*	commee-vwahzhē*r*r
What is the return limit of tickets?	*Quelle est la durée de validité des billets?*	kel a*i* lah dêureh de*r* valeedeeteh da*i* bee'ya*i*
Are stop-overs allowed?	*Est-il permis d'arrêter en cours de route?*	a*i*-teel pa*i*rmee darra*i*teh ah**n** coor de*r* root
Stop-overs are allowed at all points en route	*Il est permis d'arrêter à toutes les stations sur le parcours*	eel a*i* pa*i*rmee darra*i*teh ah toot la*i* stahs'yo**n**s sêur le*r* pahrcoor
Does a child . . . years of age require a ticket?	*Est-ce qu'il faut un billet pour un enfant de . . . ans?*	ess keel foht u**n** bee'ya*i* poor ̂e*r*n ̂ah**n**fah**n** de*r* . . . ah**n**
Children 5 years of age and under 12 pay half fare. Under five years of age when accompanied by parent or guardian, they travel free	*Les enfants de 5 a 12 ans paient demi-place. Ceux de moins de 5 ans voyagent gratuitement lorsqu'ils sont accompagnés d'un parent ou gardien*	laiz ̂ah**n**fah**n** de*r* sank ̂ah dooz ̂ah**n** pa*i* de*r*mee-plahss. sē*r* de*r* mwan de*r* sank ̂ah**n** vwayahzh' gratêueet' mah**n** kah**n**t ̂eel so**n**t ̂ acco**n**panyeh du**n** parah**n** oo gahrdy'a**n**
I want a ticket to . . .	*Je voudrais un billet pour*	zhe*r* voodraiz ̂u**n** beeya*i* poor . . .
Would you care to buy a parlour car seat?	*Voulez-vous un fauteuil de wagon-salon?*	vooleh-vooz ̂u**n** fohtēree de*r* vahgo**n**-sahlo**n**?
a lower berth	*un lit du bas*	u**n** lee dêu bah
an upper berth	*un lit du haut*	u**n** lee dêu oh
a compartment	*un compartiment*	u**n** co**n**pahrteemah**n**

English	French	Pronunciation
a drawing room	*un salon-lits*	**un** salon-lee
a bedroom	*une chambrette*	eûn shah**n**brett
What class please? [ing?]	*Première classe ou touriste?*	pre*r*mya*i*r clahss oo tooreest
When are you leav-	*Quand partez-vous?*	kah**n** pahrteh-voo?
This morning	*Ce matin*	se*r* mata**n**
At noon	*A midi*	ah meedee
This afternoon	*Cet après-midi*	set^ahpra*i*-meedee
Tonight	*Ce soir*	se*r* swar
Tomorrow morning	*Demain matin*	de*r*ma**n** mata**n**
Tomorrow noon	*Demain midi*	de*r*ma**n** meedee
Tomorrow afternoon	*Demain après-midi*	de*r*ma**n** ahpra*i*-meedee
Tomorrow night	*Demain soir*	de*r*ma**n** swar
The day after to-morrow	*Après-demain*	ahpra*i*-de*r*ma**n**
The cost is . . dollars . . . cents, please.	*Le montant s'élève à . . . dollars. . . sous*	le*r* mo**n**tahn sehla*i*v^ah . . . dollahr . . . soo
At what time is sleeper ready for occupancy?	*A quelle heure peut-on occuper le wagon-lits?*	ah kel e**rr** pe**r**t-on oc-keûpeh le*r* vagon-lee?
At . . .	*A . . .*	ah . . .
How much baggage is checked free?	*Combien de bagages peut-on faire enregistrer en franchise?*	co**n**by'a**n** de*r* bagahzh pe**r**t-on fair ahnrerzheestreh ah**n** frahn-sheez?
150 lbs. on each adult ticket and 75 lbs. on each half ticket	*Chaque billet d'adulte donne droit à cent cinquante livres et chaque demi-billet à soixante-quinze livres*	shahk beeya*i* dadeûlt dunn drwah ah sah**n** sa**n**kahnt leevr' eh shahk de*r*mi-beeya*i* ah swazah**n**t' ka**n**z leevr'
If I purchase a regular standard return ticket and use it one way, can I get a refund on the unused portion?	*Si je prends un billet d'aller et retour et ne m'en sers que dans une direction, pourrais-je obtenir un remboursement de la partie non utilisée?*	see je*r* prahnz^un beeya*i* dalleh eh re*r*toor eh ner mahn sa*i*r ke*r* dahnz^eûn deerecs'yon, poorrai-zher opt'neer u**n** rahn-boors'mahn de*r* lah pahrtee no**n** eûteeleezeh

Italic r and i silent; thick n indicates nasal; apostrophe indicates suppressed vowel.

English	French	Pronunciation
Yes Sir, you can obtain a refund on the unused portion	Oui Monsieur, vous pouvez obtenir le remboursement de la partie non utilisée	Wee, mer syēr, voo poo-vehz^opt'neer ler rahnboors'mahn der lah pahrtee non ēutee-leezeh?
What is the difference between a first class ticket and a coach ticket?	Quelle est la différence entre un billet de première classe et un billet voiture ordinaire?	kel^ai lah deefehrahnss ahntr^un bee'yai der prermyair clahss eh un beeyai vwahtēur ordeenair.
A first class Standard ticket will be accepted in sleeping or parlor cars on payment of sleeping or parlor care fare. Coach tickets are good in coaches only	Un billet de première classe permet de voyager en wagon-lits ou en wagon-salon sur paiement du prix de location ordinaire, tandis qu'un billet voiture ordinaire n'est valable que dans les voitures ordinaires	un beeyai der prermyair clahss pairmai der vwahyahzhehahn vah-gon-lee oo ahn vagon-sahlon sēur paimahn dēu pree der locah-s'yon ordeenair tahn-deess kun beeyai vwahtēur ordeenair nai valahbl' ker dahn lai vwahtēur ordeenair
I have my ticket and reservation for Quebec tonight, but I would like to reserve accommodation coming back tomorrow night	J'ai mes billets de parcours et de wagon-lits pour Québec ce soir, mais je voudrais retenir ma place de wagon-lits pour revenir demain soir	zhai mai beeyai der pahr-coor eh der vagon-lee poor kehbek ser swar, mai zher voodrai rer-t'neer mah plahss der vagon-lee poor rerv'-neer derman swar
Certainly, we will be glad to arrange it for you	Certainement, il nous fera plaisir de retenir votre place de wagon-lits	saitain'mahn, eel noo f'ra plaizeer der rer-t'neer votr' plahss der vahgon-lee
How far in advance is it necessary to make reservations?	Combien de temps à l'avance faut-il retenir ses places?	conb'yan der tahn ah lavahnss foht-eel rer-t'neer sai plahss
It is advisable to make reservations as early as possible	Il vaudrait mieux retenir vos places le plus tôt possible	eel vohdrai m'yēr rer-t'neer voh plahss ler plēu toh posseebl'

Italic r and i silent; thick n indicates nasal; apostrophe indicates suppressed vowel.

English	French	Pronunciation
What is the difference between a section and a double bedroom for two persons?	Quelle est la différence entre une section et une chambrette double pour deux personnes?	Kel︵ai lah deefehrahnss ahntr' eūn seks'yon ai eūn shahnbrett doobl' poor dēr pairsunn
A section comprises a lower and upper berth in the body of the car. A double bedroom is a small private room with a single lower and upper berth with washstand and toilet.	Une section comprend deux lits superposés dans le dortoir et une chambrette double est une petite chambre privée renfermant deux lits simples superposés, avec lavabo et aisance	eūn seks'yon conprahn dēr lee seūpairpohzeh dahn ler dortwahr ai eūn shahnbrett doobl' ait︵eūn perteet shahnbr' preeveh rahnfairmahn der lee sanpl' seūpairpohseh, avek lavahboh ai aizahnss
Can I buy a sleeper or parlor car seat on a coach class ticket?	Puis-je prendre un billet de wagon-lits ou wagon-salon avec un billet de voiture ordinaire?	peūee-zher prahndr︵un bee'yai der vahgon-lee oo vahgon-sahlon avek︵un bee'yai der vwahteūr ohrdeenair
No Sir. Coach class tickets are not good in sleeping or parlor cars	Non Monsieur. Les billets classe voiture ordinaire ne sont pas valables en wagon-lits ni en wagon-salon	non, mers'yēr. lai bee'yai clahss vwahteūr ohrdeenair ner son pah valahbl' ahn vahgon-lee nee ahn vahgon-sahlon
Do I save anything by buying a return ticket?	Y a-t-il avantage à acheter un billet d'aller et retour?	yahteel avahntahzh ah ash'teh un bee'yai d'alleh ai r'toor?
Yes, Sir, you do	Oui Monsieur	wee mers'yēr
Can I stop over on a return ticket?	Peut-on arrêter en cours de route avec un billet d'aller et retour?	pērt-on arraiteh ahn coor der root avek︵un bee'yai dalleh ai r'toor
Return tickets, with the exception of local excursion and week-end tickets, are good to stop over	Les billets d'aller et retour, sauf ceux d'excursions et de fin de semaine, permettent d'arrêter en cours de route	lai bee'yai dalleh ai r'toor, sohf sēr dexkeūs'yon ai der fan der sermain, pairmett darraiteh ahn coor der root

Italic r and i silent; thick n indicates nasal; apostrophe indicates suppressed vowel.

English	French	Pronunciation
Will you have any excursions for (Easter) (Christmas) (New Year's), etc.?	*Aurez-vous des prix réduits à l'occasion de (Pâques) (Noël) (le Jour de l'An), etc.?*	ohreh-voo dai pree reh-dēūee ah l'occahz'yon der (pahk) (noell) (lerzhoor der lahn), etc.
Yes Sir, we will have excursions for (Easter), etc.	*Oui Monsieur, nous aurons des prix réduits à l'occasion de (Pâques), etc.*	wee, mers'yēr, nooz ̂ ohron dai pree reh-dēūee ah loccahz'yon der (pahk), etc.
What is the limit on a week-end ticket?	*Quelle est la durée de validité des billets de fin de semaine?*	kel ai lah dēūreh der va-leedeeteh dai bee'yai der fan der sermain
A week-end ticket is good going from Friday noon until 2.00 p.m. Sunday, and good to return until midnight Monday following date of sale	*Les billets de fin de semaine sont bons pour partir depuis midi, le vendredi, jusqu'à deux heures p.m. le dimanche, et le voyage de retour doit commencer avant minuit, le lundi suivant*	lai bee'yai der fan der sermain son bon poor pahrteer der pēūee mee-dee ler vahndrerdee zhéūskah dērz ̂ēr pai emm ler deemahnsh, ai ler vwa'yahzh der r'toor dwah com-mahnsseh avahn mee-nēūee ler lundee sēū-eevahn
How long does it take to get to Vancouver?	*Quelle est la durée du trajet de Montréal à Vancouver?*	kel'ai lah dēūreh dēū trahzhai der monreh-ahl ah Vancouver?
Train leaving at 7.35 p.m. daily reaches there in 88 hours	*Le train quitte Montréal à 7.35 p.m. tous les jours et effectue le trajet en 88 heures*	ler tran keet monrehahl ah set ̂ērr trahnt sank pai emm too lai zhoor ai effektēū ler trahzhai ahn katr'van ērr
What is the mileage between Montreal and Vancouver?	*Quelle est la distance entre Montréal et Vancouver?*	kel ̂ai lah deestahnss ahntr monrehahl ai vancouver
2883 miles from Montreal by main line direct	*2883 milles de Montréal par itinéraire direct*	dēr meel ēūee sahn katr'-van trwah meel pahr eeteenehrair deerekt

---

Italic *r* and *i* silent; thick **n** indicates nasal; apostrophe indicates suppressed vowel.

English	French	Pronunciation
What is the difference between a standard and tourist sleeper?	*Quelle est la différence entre le wagon-lits de première et le wagon-lits touriste?*	kel'*ai* lah deefehrahnss ahntr' le*r* vahgon-lee de*r* prerm'y*ai*r clahss *ai* le*r* vahgon-lee tooreest?
To purchase accommodation on a standard sleeping car a first class ticket is required. Accommodations on a tourist sleeping car may be purchased on presentation of a coach tourist class ticket, of course, at an extra cost	*Pour occuper le wagon-lits de première il faut un billet de première classe, tandis qu'on peut occuper le wagon-lits touriste avec un billet voiture ordinaire touriste, naturellement, le prix de location est en sus.*	poor ok*eu*peh le*r* vahgon-lee de*r* prerm'y*ai*r eel foht^un bee'y*ai* de*r* prerm'y*ai*r clahss, tahndee kon p*e*rt ok*eu*peh le*r* vahgon-lee tooreest avek^un bee'y*ai* vwaht*eu*r ohrdeenair tooreest, naht*eu*rell'mahn, le*r* pree de*r* locas'yon *ai*t ahn s*eu*ss
What is the difference in cost of a standard sleeping car berth and a tourist sleeping car berth?	*Quelle différence y a-t-il entre le prix de location d'un lit dans le wagon-lits de première et le wagon-lits touriste?*	kel deefehrahnss yateel ahntr' le*r* pree de*r* locas'yon dun lee dahn le*r* vahgon-lee de*r* prerm'y*ai*r *ai* le*r* vahgon-lee tooreest?
A tourist sleeping car berth is 40% less than the cost of a standard sleeping car berth	*Un lit dans le touriste coûte 40% de moins que dans le wagon-lits de première*	un lee dahn le*r* tooreest coot karahnt poor sahn mwan ke*r* dahn le*r* vahgon-lee de*r* prerm'y*ai*r
Can I prepay a ticket for my brother from Toronto to Montreal?	*Est-ce que je puis faire délivrer un billet à mon frère, de Toronto à Montréal?*	ess ke*r* zher p*eu*ee fa*i*r dehleevreh un bee'y*ai* ah mon frair, de*r* toronto ah monreh'ahl?
Yes Sir, we will be glad to attend to that for you	*Oui Monsieur, nous serons heureux de lui faire délivrer un billet*	wee, mers'y*e*r, noo s'ron h*e*rr*e*r de*r* l*eu*ee fa*i*r dehleevreh un bee'y*ai*

Italic *r* and *i* silent; thick **n** indicates nasal; apostrophe indicates suppressed vowel.

English	French	Pronunciation
What is the cost of a bedroom from Montreal to New York?	*Quel est le prix de location d'une chambrette de Montréal à New York?*	kel^a*i* le*r* pree de*r* loca-s'yon deûn shahn-brett de*r* monreh'ahl ah New York?
The cost of single or double bedroom for one person, Montreal to New York, is $4.50, plus 45c. Canadian Government tax. A double bedroom for two persons is $5.00 plus 50c. tax	*Le prix d'une chambrette simple ou double pour une personne de Montréal à New York est $4.50, plus 45c. pour la taxe du Gouvernement. Une chambrette double pour deux personnes coûte $5, plus la taxe de 50c.*	le*r* pree deûn shahnbrett sanpl' oo doobl' de*r* monreh'ahl ah New York a*i* katr' dollahr sankahnt, pleûss ka-rahnt-sank soo poor lah tax deû goovai*r*n'-mahn. eûn shahn-brett doobl' poor dê*r* pai*r*sunn coot san dol-lahr pleûss la tax de*r* sankahnt soo
Where can I buy travellers' cheques?	*Où pourrais-je obtenir des chèques de voyageurs?*	oo poorra*i*-zhe*r* obte*r*neer da*i* sha*i*k de*r* vwa'-yahzh?
You can buy Canadian Pacific travellers' cheques and money orders right here, Sir, or from any Company's Agencies	*Vous pouvez obtenir des cheques de voyageurs du Pacifique Canadien ainsi que des mandats express ici même, Monsieur, ou de toute agence de la compagnie*	voo poovehz^opte*r*neer da*i* sha*i*k de*r* vwa'-yahzhêrr deû passee-feek canahd'yan ans-see ke*r* da*i* mahndah express eessee ma*i*m, mers'yê*r*, oo de*r* toot azhahnss de*r* lah con-pahnyee
At what station in Chicago does the Canadian Pacific train arrive?	*A quelle gare à Chicago les trains du Pacifique Canadien arrivent-t-ils?*	ah kel gahr ah sheecah-goh la*i* tran deû pas-seefeek canahd'yan arreev-teel?
At Michigan Central Depot, called Central Station	*A la gare du Michigan Central, connue sous le nom de Central Station*	ah lah gahr deû Michi-gan Central, conneû soo le*r* non de*r* Cen-tral Station
Can I take my dog in the coach?	*Puis-je prendre mon chien avec moi dans la voiture ordinaire?*	peûee-zhe*r* prahndr' mon sh'yan avek mwah dahn lah vwah-teûr ohrdeena*i*r?

Italic *r* and *i* silent; thick **n** indicates nasal; apostrophe indicates suppressed vowel.

English	French	Pronunciation
No Sir, only in compartments or drawing rooms	Non Monsieur, les chiens ne sont admis que dans les compartiments et les salon-lits	non, mers'yēr, lai sh'yan ner son pah admee ker dahn lai conpahrteemahn ai lai sahlon-lee
Can I check skis on the train?	Peut-on faire enregistrer des skis?	pērt-on fair ahnrerzhee-streh dai skee?
Skis may be checked on regular trains, but not on excursion trains	Les skis peuvent être expédiés dans les trains réguliers, mais non dans les trains d'excursions	lai skee pērvt^aitr' expehd'yeh dahn lai tran rehgheul'yeh, mai non dahn lai tran dexkéurs'yon
How long is a return ticket good for?	Quelle est la durée de validité des billets d'aller et retour?	kel^ai lah dēureh der valeedeeteh dai bee'yai dalleh ai r'toor?
A regular return ticket is good for six months from date of issue	Les billets d'aller et retour sont bons pour six mois	lai bee'yai dalleh ai r'toor son bon poor see mwah
Can I have my baggage examined in Montreal before leaving for the United States?	Peut-on faire examiner ses bagages à Montréal en partant pour les Etats-Unis?	pērt-on fair exameeneh sai bagahzh ah monreh'ahl ahn partahn poor laiz^ehtahz^eunee?
You may have your baggage examined by United States Customs Officers at Windsor Station before departure	On peut faire examiner ses bagages par l'officier des douanes des Etats-Unis à la gare Windsor, avant le départ	on pēr fair exameeneh sai bagahzh pahr loffeess'yeh dai dwahn daiz^ehtahz^eunee ah lah gahr der windsor, avahn ler dehpahr
If I purchase a tourist sleeping car ticket, can I eat in the diner?	Est-ce que les voyageurs en wagon-lits touriste, peuvent prendre leurs repas dans le wagon-restaurant	ess ker lai vwa'yahzhērr ahn vahgon-lee tooreest, pērv prahndr' lērr rerpah dahn ler vahgon-restohrahn?
Yes Sir	Oui Monsieur	wee, mērs'yēr

Italic r and i silent; thick n indicates nasal; apostrophe indicates suppressed vowel.

English	French	Pronunciation
Will you place my name on the waiting list for lower, bedroom compartment, drawing room, etc.?	*Voulez-vous mettre mon nom sur la liste pour un lit du bas, une chambrette, un compartiment, un salon-lits?*	vooleh-voo mettr' mon non seūr lah leest poor un lee deū bah, eūn shahnbrett, un conpahrteemahn, un sahlon-lee?
Yes, Sir	*Oui Monsieur, voulez-vous me dire votre nom et votre numéro de téléphone?*	wee, mers'yēr, voolehvoo mer deer votr' non ai votr' neūmehroh der tehlehfohn?
Is it necessary to have a passport for travel to Europe?	*Faut-il un passeport pour voyager en Europe?*	foht-il^un pahss-pohr poor vwa'yahzheh ahn ērrop?
Yes Sir	*Oui Monsieur*	wee, mers'yēr
To whom do I apply for a passport?	*A qui faut-il s'adresser pour obtenir un passeport?*	ah kee foht-eel sadresseh poor^opterneer un pahss-pohr?
If you are British born you may apply to the Dominion Passport Officer at Ottawa	*Si vous êtes sujet britannique de naissance, vous pouvez vous adresser "au Chef du Service des passeports, Ministère des Affaires Extérieures, Ottawa*	see vooz^ait seūzhai breetanneek der naissahnss, voo pooveh vooz^adresseh "oh shef deū sairveess dai pahss-pohr, meeneestair daiz^affairz^extehr'yērr, Ottawa"

In the Hotel Front Office

English	French	Pronunciation
How do you do?	*Comment allez-vous?*	commahnt^alleh-voo?
What are your rates?	*Quels sont vos taux?*	kels son voh toh?
I believe you have a reservation for me	*Je crois que vous avez une chambre réservée pour moi*	zher crwah ker vooz^ aveh eūn shahnbr' rehsairveh poor mwah
Have you a room with a shower?	*Avez-vous une chambre avec douche?*	aveh-vooz^eūn shanbr' avek doosh
What is the rate on this room?	*Quel est le prix de cette chambre?*	kel ai ler pree der set shahnbr'?

Italic *r* and *i* silent; thick **n** indicates nasal; apostrophe indicates suppressed vowel.

English	French	Pronunciation
Can you give me two rooms with a connecting bath?	*Pouvez-vous me donner deux chambres avec salle de bain communicante?*	pooveh-voo mer dunneh dēr shahnbr' avek sahl der ban commēuneecahnt?
I would like to have two connecting rooms with a parlor	*Je désirerais deux chambres communicantes avec un salon*	zher dehzeer'rai dēr shahnbr commēuneecahnt avek un sahlon
Can I have a room without bath?	*Puis-je avoir une chambre avec salle de bain?*	pēuee-zher avwahr ēun shahnbr avek sahl der ban
I would like to have one double room with bath and one without bath	*Je voudrais une chambre double avec salle de bain, et une sans salle de bain*	zher voo-draiz^ēun shahnbr doobl avek sahl der ban, ai ēun sahn sahl der ban
Can you give me two rooms on the same floor?	*Pouvez-vous me donner deux chambres sur le même étage?*	pooveh-voo mer dunneh dēr shahnbr sēur ler maim ehtahzh?
Will you please keep a room next to mine for a friend who is arriving this afternoon?	*Voulez-vous, s'il-vous-plaît, réserver une chambre près de la mienne pour un ami qui doit arriver cet après-midi?*	vooleh-voo seel voo plai rehzairveh ēun shahnbr prai der lah m'yenn poor un ahmee kee dwaht arreeveh set aprai-meedee
I would like to change my room to one facing the river	*Je désirerais changer ma chambre pour une autre donnant sur le fleuve*	zher dehzeer'rai shahnzheh mah shahnbr poor ēun ohtr' dunnahn sēur ler flērv'
What is the difference in rate?	*Quelle différence y a-t-il dans le prix?*	kel deeffehrahnss yahteel dahn ler pree?
What are your rates on double and single rooms?	*Quels sont les prix de vos chambres doubles et simples?*	kels son lai pree der voh shahnbr doobl' ai sanpl'?
The boy has your key	*Le garçon a votre clef*	ler gahrsson ah votre cleh
What is my room number?	*Quel est le numéro de ma chambre?*	kel ai ler nēumehroh der mah shahnbr

Italic *r* and *i* silent; thick **n** indicates nasal; apostrophe indicates suppressed vowel.

English	French	Pronunciation
How many days do you expect to be here?	*Combien de jours pensez-vous être ici?*	conb'yan der zhoor pahnseh-voo aitr' eessee
Give me the key to my room	*Donnez-moi la clef de ma chambre*	dunneh-mwah lah cleh der mah shahnbr
Where are your house phones?	*Où sont les téléphones de l'hôtel?*	oo son lai tehlehfohn der lohtel?
Where can I send a telegram?	*Où puis-je envoyer un télégramme?*	oo peüee-zher ahnvwah'-yeh un tehlehgram
Where is your main dining-room?	*Où est votre salle à manger principale?*	oo ai votr' sahl ah mahnzheh pranseepahl?
I expect to stay with you for two weeks	*Je compte rester ici deux semaines*	zher cont' raisteh eesee dēr s'main
Please cancel my reservation	*S'il-vous-plaît, annulez ma location*	seel voo plai annéuleh mah locas'yon
Please see to it that my name does not appear in newspapers	*Veuillez voir à ce que mon nom n'apparaisse pas dans les journaux*	vēryeh vwahr ah ser ker mon non nappahraiss pah dahn lai zhoornoh
Please make reservation for my return next week	*Veuillez retenir une chambre pour mon retour la semaine prochaine*	vēryeh rert'neer éun shahnbr' poor mon rertoor lah s'main proshain
Where is the Manager's office?	*Où est le bureau du Gérant?*	oo ai ler beüroh déu zhehrahn?
Where is the barber shop located?	*Où est situé le salon de barbier?*	oo ai seetéueh ler sahlon der bahrb'yeh?
What is your commercial rate?	*Quel est votre tarif commercial?*	kel ai votr' tahreef commairs'yahl
I wish to pay for my room in advance	*Je désire payer ma chambre d'avance*	zher dehzeer pai'yeh mah shahnbr davahnss
Please change my reservation to Friday instead of Thursday	*Veuillez réserver pour vendredi au lieu de jeudi*	vēryeh rehzairveh poor vahndrerdee oh lyēr der zhērdee
Good morning, sir	*Bonjour, monsieur*	bonzhoor, mersyēr
What is the weather like to-day?	*Quelle température fait-il aujourd'hui?*	kel tahnpehrahtéur fait-eel ohzhoordéuee?

Italic *r* and *i* silent; thick **n** indicates nasal; apostrophe indicates suppressed vowel.

English	French	Pronunciation
Is there anything in my box?	*Y a-t-il quelque chose dans mon casier?*	yahteel kelker shohz dahn mon cahz'yeh?
At what time must I check out so as not to pay for an extra day?	*A quelle heure dois-je remettre ma chambre pour ne pas payer une journée de plus?*	ah kel ērr dwah-zher rermettr' ma shanbr poor ner pah pai'yeh ēun zhoorneh der plēu?
Will you send a boy for my baggage?	*Voulez-vous envoyer un garçon prendre mes bagages?*	vooleh-vooz ahnvwah'yeh un gahrsson prahndr mai bagahzh
Please let me have what is in my box	*Veuillez me donner ce qu'il y a dans mon casier*	vēryeh mer dunneh ser keelyah dahn mon caz'yeh
Please have your porter put sample tables in my room	*Veuillez s'il-vous-plait faire mettre des tables d'échantillons dans ma chambre par le portier*	vēryeh seel voo plai fair mettr' dai tahbl' dehshahntee'yon dahn mah shahnbr' pahr ler pohrt'yeh
Will you have me called at seven o'clock in the morning?	*Voulez-vous me faire appeler demain matin à sept heures?*	vooleh-voo mer fair app'leh d'man matan ah set^ērr?
Where is your telegraph office?	*Où est votre bureau de télégraphe?*	oo ai votr' bēuroh der telehgrahf?
Where do I buy stamps?	*Où puis-je acheter des timbres?*	oo pēuee-zh' assh'teh dai tanbr'?
Where is the nearest church?	*Où est située l'église la plus proche?*	oo ai seetēueh lehgleez lah plēu prosh?
Where can I get a bottle of liquor?	*Où puis-je avoir une bouteille de liqueur?*	oo pēuee-zh' avwahr ēun bootaiee der leekērr?
Where do I get money changed?	*Où puis-je faire changer de l'argent?*	oo pēuee-zher fair shahnzheh der lahrzhahn?
What is the difference between a nine and a twelve dollar room?	*Quelle est la différence entre une chambre de neuf et de douze dollars?*	kel ai lah deefehrahnss ahntr' ēun shahnbr der nērf ai der dooz dollahr

Italic *r* and *i* silent; thick n indicates nasal; apostrophe indicates suppressed vowel.

English	French	Pronunciation
Will I register for my friend?	*Dois-je enregistrer mon ami?*	dwah-zher ahnrerzhees-treh mon ami
What times does the orchestra play for dinner?	*A quelle heure joue l'orchestre pour le dîner?*	ah kel hĕrr zhoo lohr-kestr' poor ler deeneh?
Where is tea being served?	*Où est servi le thé?*	oo ai sairvee ler teh?
In what room do you have dancing?	*Dans quelle salle danse-t-on?*	dahn kel sahl dahnss-ton?
Will you have my bill ready?	*Voulez-vous faire pré-parer mon compte?*	vooleh-voo fair preh-pahreh mon cont'
What is a good hotel to stop at in Mon-treal?	*Donnez-moi le nom d'un bon hôtel à Montréal.*	dunneh-mwah ler non dun bon ˆohtel ahmon-reh'ahl
Do you make a spe-cial rate for a stay of two weeks?	*Accordez-vous une réduction pour un séjour de deux se-maines?*	accohrdeh-vooz eŭn reh-deŭks'yon poor un seh-zhoor der dēr s'main?
Have you any mail for me?	*Avez-vous du courrier pour moi?*	aveh-voo deŭ coor'yeh poor mwah?
Is there anything in my box?	*Est-ce qu'il y a quel-que chose dans mon casier?*	ess keel ya kelker shohz dahn mon caz'yeh
What time do you receive the next mail?	*A quelle heure re-cevez-vous le pro-chain courrier?*	ah kel ĕrr rers'veh-voo ler proshan coor'yeh?
Have you a tele-gram addressed to me?	*Avez-vous un télé-gramme pour moi?*	aveh-vooz ˆun tehleh-gram poor mwah
Will you please for-ward my mail?	*Voulez-vous s'il-vous-plaît faire suivre mon courrier?*	vooleh-voo seel voo plai fair seueevr mon coor'yeh
What is the postage of a special de-livery letter?	*Combien faut-il met-tre de timbres sur une lettre livraison spéciale?*	conb'yan foht-eel mettr der tanbr seŭr ˆeŭn lettr leevraizon spehs'yahl?
Is there air mail ser-vice from this city?	*Est-ce qu'il y a un service postal par avion de cette ville?*	ess keel ya un sairveess postahl pahr av'yon der set veel

Italic *r* and *i* silent; thick **n** indicates nasal; apostrophe indicates suppressed vowel.

English	French	Pronunciation
What time do you receive the Toronto mail?	*A quelle heure recevez-vous le courrier de Toronto?*	a kel ērr rers'veh-voo ler coor'yeh der toronto
When was this letter received?	*Quand avez-vous reçu cette lettre?*	kahntˆaveh-voo rersseū set lettr?
Please repeat telegrams to me on board the train	*Veuillez me faire répéter mes télégrammes sur le train*	vēryeh mer fair rehpeh-teh mai tehlehgram seūr ler tran
Is the morning mail in?	*Le courrier du matin est-il arrivé?*	ler coor'yeh deū matan ait-eel arreeveh?
Is the afternoon mail in?	*Le courrier de l'après-midi est-il arrivé?*	ler coor'yeh der l'aprai-meedee ait-eel arree-veh
Please hold all mail until my return	*Veuillez gardez mon courrier jusqu'à mon retour*	vēryeh gahrdeh mon coor'yeh zhéūskah mon rertoor
Can I have a safety deposit box?	*Puis-je avoir un coffret de sûreté?*	pēūee-zher avwahr un coffrai der seūr'teh?
If you receive a telegram for me will you call me at this number?	*Si vous recevez un télégramme pour moi, voulez-vous m'appeler à ce numéro?*	see voo rers'veh un teh-lehgram poor mwah, vocleh-voo mapp'leh ah ser neūmehroh
At what time is the next mail collected?	*A quelle heure est le prochain lever du courrier?*	ah kel ērr ai ler proshan lerveh deū coor'yer
We have a letter for you	*Nous avons une lettre pour vous*	noozˆavonzˆeūn lettr' poor voo
Can I have this letter registered here?	*Puis-je faire recommander cette lettre ici?*	pēūee-zher fair rercom-mahndeh set lettr' ees-see?
We have a telegram for you	*Nous avons un télégramme pour vous*	noozˆavonzˆun tehleh-gram poor voo
Shall we send it up to your room?	*Devons-nous l'envoyer à votre chambre?*	dervon-noo lahnvwah'-'yer ah votr' shahnbr?
Please return all mail to the sender	*S'il vous plaît retournez tout courrier à l'envoyeur.*	seel voo plai, rertoorneh too coor'yeh ah l'ahn-vwah'yērr

Italic *r* and *i* silent; thick **n** indicates nasal; apostrophe indicates suppressed vowel.

English	French	Pronunciation
Will you please open and read the telegram over the 'phone?	Voulez-vous ouvrir et lire le télégramme au téléphone?	vooleh-vooz^oovreer ai leer ler tehlehgram oh tehlehfohn?
Do you need extra postage to re-address and forward a letter?	Est-il nécessaire d'ajouter d'autres timbres pour réadresser et faire suivre une lettre?	ait-eel nehsessair dahzhooteh dohtr' tanbr' poor reh-adresseh ai fair seūeevr eūn lettr
Do you receive mail on Sunday?	Est-ce que vous recevez du courrier le dimanche?	ess ker voo rers'veh deū coor'yeh ler deemahnsh
Let me have a forwarding card	Veuillez me donner une carte pour faire suivre mon courrier	vĕr'yeh mer dunneh eūn cahrt poor fair seūeevr mon coor'yer
Who must I see to cash a personal cheque?	Qui dois-je voir pour changer un chèque personnel?	kee dwah-zher vwahr poor shahnzheh un shaik pairsunnel?
Where can I buy travellers' cheques?	Où puis-je acheter des chèques de voyageurs?	oo peūee-zh' ahsh'teh dai shaik der vwah-yazhĕrr?
Is American money at par?	Est-ce que l'argent américain est au pair?	ess ker l'ahrzahn ameh-reecan ait^oh pair?
Where do I leave my key?	Où dois-je laisser ma clef?	oo dwah-zher laisseh mah cleh?
Will you pay for a parcel addressed to me?	Voulez-vous payer pour un colis qui m'est adressé?	vooleh-voo pai'yeh poor un colee kee mait^ adresseh?
Will you please send the bill to my room?	Voulez-vous envoyer le compte à ma chambre?	vooleh-vooz^ahnvwah' yeh ler cont ah mah shahnbr?
Please change a dollar for me	Veuillez me donner la monnaie d'un dollar	vĕr'yeh mer dunneh lah munnai dun dollahr
Have you any American money?	Avez-vous de l'argent américain?	aveh-voo der lahrzahn amehreecan?
Can I have a cash-advance on my bill?	Pouvez-vous m'avancer de l'argent sur mon compte?	pooveh-voo mahvahnsseh der lahrzahn seūr mon cont'

Italic *r* and *i* silent; thick **n** indicates nasal; apostrophe indicates suppressed vowel.

English	French	Pronunciation
Can I charge railway tickets on my bill?	Puis-je faire charger des billets de chemin de fer sur mon compte?	peūee-zher fair shahrzheh dai bee'yai der sh'man der fair seūr mon cont
Do you charge for phone calls made from one room to another?	Faites-vous payer les appels téléphoniques d'une chambre à une autre?	fait'-voo paiyeh laizˆappel tehlehfohneek deūn shahnbr' ah eūn ohtr'
What is the amount of my last week's bill?	Quel est le montant de ma note pour la semaine dernière?	kel ai ler montahn der mah not poor lah s'main dairn'yair?
Give me my bill	Donnez-moi ma note	dunneh-mwah ma not
What time do I have to check out?	A quelle heure dois-je remettre ma chambre?	ah kel ērr dwah-zher rermettr' mah shahnbr?
Can I have my bill sent on?	Pouvez-vous m'envoyer ma note?	pooveh-voo mahnvwahyeh mah not?

In the Hotel Dining Room

What are your meal prices?	Quels sont les prix de vos repas?	kel son lai pree der voh rerpah?
Did you enjoy your dinner?	Avez-vous bien mangé?	aveh-voo b'yan mahnzheh?
Yes, thanks, I enjoyed it very much	Oui, merci, j'ai très bien dîné	wee, mairsee, zheh trai b'yan deeneh
Give me a bottle of white wine.	Donnez-moi une bouteille de vin blanc	dunneh-mwah eūn bootai'yer der van blahn
Are the meals à la carte?	Est-ce que les repas sont à la carte?	ess ker lai rerpah sontˆah lah cahrt?
We serve à la carte and if you wish there is also table d'hote at a regular price	Nous servons à la carte et, si vous le désirez, il y a aussi la table d'hôte à prix fixe	noo'sairvonzˆah lah cahrt ai see voo le dehzeereh eelyah ohssee lah tahbl' doht ah pree feex
Do you serve beer and wines with meals?	Servez-vous la bière et le vin avec les repas?	sairveh-voo lah b'yair ai ler van avek lai rērpah?
Can I have breakfast served in my room?	Puis-je me faire servir à déjeuner dans ma chambre?	peūee-zher mer fair sairveer ah dehzhērneh dahn mah shahnbr

---

Italic r and i silent; thick n indicates nasal; apostrophe indicates suppressed vowel.

English	French	Pronunciation
At what time does your dining-room open for breakfast?	A quelle heure s'ouvre la salle à manger pour le petit déjeuner?	a kel ērr soovre lah sahl ah mahnzheh poor ler pertee dehzhērneh
Will you reserve a table for four people for dinner?	Voulez-vous réserver une table pour quatre personnes pour le dîner?	vooleh-voo rehzairveh eūn tahbl poor kahtr pairsunn poor ler deeneh
I am in a hurry, where can I have a quick breakfast?	Je suis pressé, où puis-je me faire servir à déjeuner rapidement?	zher seūee presseh, oo peūee-zher mer fair sairveer ah dehzhērneh rapeed'mahn?
Can we have a lunch prepared to take along with us?	Peut-on faire préparer un lunch pour apporter avec nous?	pērt-on fair prehpahrer un lunsh poor appohrteh avek noo
I would like a table by the window.	J'aimerais avoir une table près d'une fenêtre	zhaim'raiz͡avwahr͡eūn tabl' prai deūn fernaitr'
Do you charge extra for a private dining room?	Exigez-vous un supplément pour une salle à dîner privée?	exeezheh-vooz͡un seūpplehmahn poor eūn sahl ah deeneh preeveh?
What price can you quote me for a dinner?	Quel prix pouvez-vous me faire pour un dîner?	kel pree pooveh-voo mer fair poor͡un deeneh?
Have you anything special you can suggest?	Avez-vous quelque chose de spécial à me suggérer?	aveh-voo kelker shohz der spehss'yahl ah mer seūgzhehreh?
What wine would go nicely with this dinner?	Quel vin conviendrait avec ce dîner?	kel van conv'yandrai avek ser deeneh?
Can we have hors d'œuvres and cocktails served in our bedroom or where could you serve them?	Pouvons-nous nous faire servir des hors-d'œuvre et des cocktails dans notre chambre ou à quelle place pouvez-vous les servir?	poovon-noo noo fair sairveer dai ohr-dērvr' ai dai coktail dahn notr shahnbr oo ah kel plahss pooveh-voo lai sairveer.

Italic *r* and *i* silent; thick **n** indicates nasal; apostrophe indicates suppressed vowel.

English	French	Pronunciation
What kind of meals do you serve in rooms?	*Quel genre de repas servez-vous dans les chambres?*	kel zhahnrer der rerpah sairveh-voo dahn lai shahnbr?
At what hours do you serve meals?	*A quelle heure servez-vous les repas?*	ah kel ērr sairveh-voo lai rerpah?
The dining-room is open from six-thirty in the morning until midnight and table d'hôte meals are served as follows:—	*La salle à manger est ouverte de six heures et demie à minuit et les repas table d'hôte sont servis comme suit:*	lah sahl ah mahnzheh ai-t˄oovairt der seez ērr ai d'mee ah meeneūee ai lai rerpah tahbl' doht son sairvee com seūee
Breakfast from six-thirty to ten	*Le petit déjeuner, de six heures et demie à dix*	ler pertee dehzhērneh, der seez˄ērr, ai d'mee ah deess
Luncheon from twelve to two	*Le déjeuner à la fourchette, de midi à deux heures*	ler dehzhērneh ah lah foorshett, der meedee ah dērz˄ērr
Dinner from six to nine	*Le dîner, de six à neuf heures*	ler deeneh, der seez˄ah nērv˄ērr
I would like to have hot milk with my coffee	*Je voudrais du lait chaud avec mon café*	zher voodrai deū lai shoh avek mon cahfeh

Carriage Agents

Have my car sent over to the garage	*Faites envoyer ma voiture au garage*	faitz˄ahnvwahyeh mah vwahteūr oh garahz
Can I have a guide to show me around town?	*Puis-je avoir un guide pour visiter la ville?*	peūee-zher avwahr˄un gheed poor veezeeteh lah veel
Get me a taxi	*Appelez-moi un taxi*	app'leh-mwah un taxee
How long does it take to get to the station?	*Combien faut-il de temps pour se rendre à la gare?*	conb'yan foht-eel de tahn poor ser rahndr' ah lah gahr?
Do you have a bus service to the station?	*Est-ce que vous avez un service d'autobus pour la gare?*	ess-ker vooz˄avehz˄un sairveess dohtobeūss poor lah gahr?

Italic *r* and *i* silent; thick **n** indicates nasal; apostrophe indicates suppressed vowel.

English	French	Pronunciation
Have you a garage connected with the hotel?	*Est-ce que vous avez un garage en rapport avec l'hôtel?*	ess-ke*r* vooz^avehz^ u**n** garahzh ah**n** rappohr avek lohtel?
Have my car here for seven o'clock tomorrow morning	*Faites venir ma voiture ici pour sept heures, demain matin*	fai*t* v'neer mah vwahteû*r* eessee poor set ê*r*r, d'ma**n** mata**n**
Have you seen my chauffeur?	*Avez-vous vu mon chauffeur?*	aveh-voo veû mo**n** shohfê*r*r?
Where is your tourist information bureau?	*Où est votre bureau de renseignements pour les touristes?*	oo a*i* votr' beûroh de*r* rah**n**sain'ye*r*mah**n** poor la*i* tooreest?
Where is the Museum?	*Où est situé le Musée?*	oo a*i* seetéûeh le*r* meûzeh
What is the temperature?	*Quelle est la température?*	kel a*i* la tah**n**pehrahteû*r*?
What is your population?	*Quelle est votre population?*	kel a*i* votr popeûlah-s'yo**n**?
Pay my cab	*Payez mon taxi*	pai'yeh mo**n** taxee
Where can we get information on roads?	*Où peut-on avoir des renseignements sur les routes?*	oo pê*r*t-o**n** avwahr da*i* rah**n**sain'ye*r*mah**n** seû*r* la*i* root?
Will you get me a nice car with a good chauffeur to drive around the city	*Procurez-moi une belle voiture et un bon chauffeur pour faire le tour de la ville*	prokeûreh-mwah eû**n** bel vwahteû*r* a*i* u**n** bo**n** shohfê*r*r poor fai*r* le*r* too*r* dê*r* lah veel
What is the charge per hour for a car?	*Quel est le tarif à l'heure pour une voiture?*	kel a*i* le*r* tahreef ah lê*r*r poor^eû**n** vwahteû*r*?
Are the roads in a very bad state?	*Est-ce que les routes sont dans un bien mauvais état?*	ess-ke*r* la*i* root so**n** dah**n**z^u**n** b'ya**n** mohvaiz^ehtah?
Which is the largest departmental store in the city?	*Quel est le plus grand magasin à rayons en ville?*	kel a*i* le*r* pleû grah**n** magahza**n** ah rai'yo**n** ah**n** veel?

Italic *r* and *i* silent; thick **n** indicates nasal; apostrophe indicates suppressed vowel.

Porters and Bell Boys

English	French	Pronunciation
Can I have my baggage sent to the station?	*Puis-je faire envoyer mes bagages à la gare?*	pĕuee-zher fair ahn-vwah'yeh mai bagahzh ah lah gahr
Where is the check room?	*Où est le vestiaire?*	oo ai ler vaist'yair?
Where is the ticket office?	*Où est le bureau des billets?*	oo ai ler bĕuroh dai bee' yai
Where is the drug store?	*Où est la pharmacie?*	oo ai lah fahrmahssee?
Have you a billiard room?	*Avez-vous une salle de billard?*	aveh-vooz ̂ĕun sahl der bee'yahr?
How long does it take to have a suit cleaned?	*Combien faut-il de temps pour faire nettoyer un complet?*	conb'yan foht-eel der tahn poor fair nettwah'yeh un conplai?
Do you have a one-day laundry service?	*Avez-vous un service de buanderie faisant livraison en une journée?*	aveh-vooz ̂un sairveess der bĕuahnd'ree ferzahn leevraizon ahn ĕun zhoorneh?
Can I check baggage in the hotel while I am away?	*Puis-je faire enregistrer mes bagages dans l'hôtel durant mon absence?*	pĕuee-zher fair ahnrer-zheestreh mai bagahzh dahn lohtel dĕurahn mon ̂absahnss
Where can I have my shoes repaired?	*Où puis-je faire réparer mes chaussures?*	oo pĕuee-zher fair reh-pahreh mai shohssĕur?
Will you bring me ice water?	*Voulez-vous m'apporter de l'eau à la glace?*	vooleh-voo mappohrteh der l'oh ah lah glahss?
How many trunks have you?	*Combien de malles avez-vous?*	conb'yan der mahl aveh-voo?
Have my baggage brought up immediately to my room	*Faites monter mes bagages immédiatement à ma chambre*	fait monteh mai bagahzh eemmehd'yaht' mahn ah mah shahn-br
I am leaving about nine o'clock	*Je partirai vers neuf heures*	zher pahrteereh vair nĕr ̂ĕrr

Italic *r* and *s* silent; thick **n** indicates nasal; apostrophe indicates suppressed vowel.

English	French	Pronunciation
Have my baggage brought down	*Faites descendre mes bagages*	fait dehssahndr' mai bagahzh'
What is there interesting to see in your city?	*Qu'y a-t-il d'intéressant à voir dans votre ville?*	kyat-eel dantehressahn ah vwahr dahn votr' veel?
Where is the elevator?	*Où est l'ascenseur?*	oo ai lassahnsêrr?
Where can I get writing paper?	*Où puis-je me procurer du papier à écrire?*	oo pêuee-zher mer prokêureh dêu pap'yeh ah ehcreer?
Where is the writing room?	*Où est la salle d'écriture?*	oo ai lah sahl dehcreetêur?
Where is the general delivery?	*Où est la poste restante?*	oo ai lah post restahnt?
I should like to go to a theatre	*Je voudrais aller au théâtre*	zher voodraizˆalleh oh teh-ahtr
Bring me some cigarettes	*Apportez-moi des cigarettes*	appohrteh-mwah dai seegarett
What kind do you wish, Sir?	*Quelle sorte désirez-vous, Monsieur?*	kel sohrt dehzeereh-voo, mers'yêr
Is it cold enough for an overcoat?	*Fait-il assez froid pour porter un pardessus?*	fait-eel asseh frwah poor pohrteh un pahrd'sêu?
Where can I buy a good pair of shoes?	*Où puis-je acheter une bonne paire de chaussures?*	oo pêuee-zher ahsh'teh êun bon pair der shohssêur?
Have you any night clubs?	*Y a-t-il des clubs de nuit?*	yateel dai clêub der nêuee?
I am going to the United States—is it necessary to have my trunks examined?	*Je vais aux Etats-Unis; est-il nécessaire de faire examiner mes malles?*	zher vai ohzˆehtahzˆêunee; ait-eel nehssessair der fair exameeneh mai mahl?
Please have my coat and hat checked	*Veuillez s'il vous plaît prendre mon paletot et mon chapeau en consigne*	vêr'yeh seel voo plai prahndr' mon pahl'toh ai mon shapoh ahn conseen'yer
Will you bring down my laundry	*Voulez-vous apporter mon linge?*	vooleh-voozˆappohrteh mon lanzh?

Italic *r* and *i* silent; thick **n** indicates nasal; apostrophe indicates suppressed vowel.

English	French	Pronunciation
I am leaving tomorrow morning	*Je pars demain matin*	zher pahr derma**n** mata**n**
Where is the registration desk?	*Où est le bureau d'enregistrement?*	oo a*i* le*r* be*u*roh dah**n**-rerzheestr'mah**n**?
Where is the cashier's wicket?	*Où est le guichet du caissier?*	oo a*i* le*r* gheesha*i* de*u* caiss'yeh?

Housekeeper's Department

Will you have my room made up?	*Voulez-vous faire ma chambre?*	vooleh-voo fai*r* mah shah**n**br'?
Send the maid to my room	*Voulez-vous m'envoyer la fille de chambre?*	vooleh-voo mah**n**vwah'-yeh lah fee'ye*r* de*r* shah**n**br'?
May I have more towels?	*Puis-je avoir d'autres serviettes?*	pe*u*eezh'avwahr dohtr' sairv'yett
Put an extra blanket on my bed	*Mettez une couverture de plus sur mon lit*	mettehz'e*u*n coovairte*u*r der ple*u* se*u*r mon lee
May I have an extra pillow?	*Puis-je avoir un oreiller de plus?*	pe*u*eezh' avwahr e*r*n^oh-rai'yeh der ple*u*?
May I have more writing paper?	*Puis-je avoir plus de papier à écrire?*	pe*u*eezh' avwahr ple*u* der pahp'yeh ah eh-creer?
Will you lock my door?	*Voulez-vous fermer ma porte à clef?*	vooleh-voo fai*r*meh mah pohrt ah cleh?
Will you unlock my door?	*Voulez-vous ouvrir ma porte?*	vooleh-vooz^oovreer mah pohrt?
Who will take my laundry down?	*Qui va descendre mon linge à la buanderie?*	kee vah da*i*sahndr' mon lah**n**zh ah lah be*u*ahn-d'ree?
Will you give me more matches?	*Voulez-vous me donner d'autres allumettes?*	vooleh-voo me*r* donneh dohtrerz^alle*u*mett?
I would like more soap	*Je désirerais plus de savon*	zhe*r* dehzeer'ra*i* ple*u* de*r* sahvo**n**
Where do I ring for the maid?	*Où dois-je sonner pour la fille de chambre?*	oo dwah-zher sonneh poor lah fee'ye*r* der shah**n**br?
If any one knocks on my door, tell them I am down stairs	*Si quelqu'un frappe à ma porte, dites que je suis en bas*	see kelku**n** frahp ah mah pohrt, deet ke*r* zhe*r* se*u*eez^ah**n** bah

Italic *r* and *i* silent; thick **n** indicates nasal; apostrophe indicates suppressed vowel.

English	French	Pronunciation
I do not wish to be disturbed	*Je ne veux pas être dérangé*	zher ner vēr pahz͡aitr dehrahnzheh
I would like to have more heat in my room	*Je désirerais avoir plus de chaleur dans ma chambre*	zher dehzeer'raiz͡avwahr plēu der shahlērr dahn mah shahnbr
Can I have stronger lights in my room?	*Puis-je avoir des lampes plus fortes dans ma chambre?*	pēueezh' avwahr dai lahnp plēu fohrt dahn mah shahnbr
Can I have an extra chair in my room?	*Puis-je avoir une chaise de plus dans ma chambre?*	pēueezh' avwahr ēun shaiz der plēu dahn ma shahnbr
Please have one of the beds taken out of this room	*Veuillez enlever un des lits de cette chambre*	vēr'yehz͡ahnl've un dai lee der set shahnbr
Please get me more coat hangers	*Procurez-moi, s'il vous plaît, d'autres supports pour complets*	prokēureh-mwah seel voo plai dohtr sēuppohrt poor conplai
Will you please have a card table sent up to my room?	*Voulez-vous s'il vous plaît me faire monter une table à cartes?*	vooleh-voo seel voo plai mer fair monteh ēun tahbl' ah cahrt?
Will you please put a cot in my room?	*Voulez-vous s'il vous plaît faire mettre un lit d'enfant dans ma chamber?*	vooleh-voo seel voo plai fair mettr un lee dahn-fahn dahn mah shahnbr
Will you please put a crib in this room?	*Voulez-vous, s'il vous plaît, mettre un berceau dans cette chambre?*	vooleh-voo seel voo plai mettr un bairsoh dahn set shahnbr?

In a Telegraph Office

What will be the cost to wire $100.00?	*Combien en coûte-t-il pour télégraphier $100.00?*	conb'yan ahn coot'-teel poor tehlehgraf'yeh san dollahr?
How long does it take for delivery of same?	*Dans combien de temps pouvez-vous en faire la livraison?*	dahn conb'yan der tahn pooveh-vooz͡ahn fair' lah leevraizon?

Italic *r* and *i* silent; thick **n** indicates nasal; apostrophe indicates suppressed vowel.

English	French	Pronunciation
Approximately one hour	*Dans une heure, approximativement*	dahnz^eun ērr, approxeemahteev'mahn
Have you a money transfer on hand for me?	*Avez-vous un transfert d'argent pour moi?*	avveh-vooz^un trahnsfair dahrzhahn poor mwah?
No, we have not; will you kindly leave your address?	*Non, nous n'en avons pas. Veuillez nous laisser votre adresse*	non, noo nahn'avon pah veree'yeh noo laisseh votr' adress
What is your name, please?	*Quel est votre nom, s'il vous plaît?*	kel^ai votr' non, seel voo plai?
Who is the sender of this money?	*Quel est le nom de l'expéditeur?*	kel^ai ler non der l'expehdeetērr?
What is the amount you are expecting?	*Quel est le montant que vous attendez?*	kel^ai ler montahn ker vooz^attahndeh?
It is necessary that you identify yourself	*Votre identification est nécessaire*	votr' eedahnteefeecass'yon ai nehsessair
Have you any papers, letters, cards, etc., for this purpose?	*Avez-vous des papiers, lettres, cartes, pour servir à votre identification?*	avveh-voo dai pap'yeh, lettr', cahrt', poor sairveer ah votr' eedahnteefeecass'yon?
Personal identification is required, you must be identified by someone known to this office, our Agent, etc.	*L'identification personnelle est nécessaire. Vous devez être identifié par quelqu'un connu de notre bureau ou par l'Agent*	l'eedahnteefeecass'yon pairsunnell ai nehsssessair voo dervehz^aitr eedahnteef'yeh pahr kelkun conneû der notr' beûroh oo pahr lahzhahn
Am ill and unable to call for money transfer	*Je suis malade et incapable d'aller chercher le transfert d'argent*	zher seûee malahd ai ancapahbl' dalleh shairsher ler trahnsfair dahrzhahn
Is it possible for you to deliver money to my home?	*Pouvez-vous le faire délivrer à ma résidence?*	pooveh-voo ler fair dehleevreh ah mah rehzeedahnss?

Italic *r* and *i* silent; thick **n** indicates nasal; apostrophe indicates suppressed vowel.

English	French	Pronunciation
We cannot deliver the cash. However, we can send you an express order	*Nous ne pouvons vous le délivrer en espèces, mais nous pouvons vous faire parvenir un mandat postal*	noo ner poovo**n** voo ler dehleevreh ahn espai*ss* mai noo poovon voo fair pahrv'neer u**n** mah**n**dah postahl
If I send a telegram and it is reported undelivered, do I have to pay for same?	*Si j'expédie un télégramme et qu'il n'est pas délivré, dois-je en payer les frais?*	see zhexpehdee u**n** tehlehgram ai keel nai pah dehleevreh, dwahzher ah**n** pai'yeh lai frai
Yes, you have to pay regardless	*Oui, vous devez payer les frais*	wee, voo derveh pai'yeh lai frai
If I send a message collect and charges are refused by addressee, do I have to pay for same?	*Si j'expédie un message dont les frais devront être payés par le destinataire et qu'il refuse de le faire, en suis-je responsable?*	see zhexpehdee u**n** messahzh do**n** lai frai dervro**n**t ^ aitr' pai'yeh pahr ler daisteenahtai ai keel rerfeuz' der ler fair, ah**n** seuee-zher rerspo**n**sabl?
Yes, the sender of collect telegrams is responsible for charges	*Oui, l'expéditeur est responsable des frais si le destinataire refuse de les payer*	wee, lexpehdeeterr ai rerspo**n**sabl' dai frai see ler daisteenahtair rerfeuz der lai pai'yeh
I want a message repeated, whom do I ask for?	*A qui dois-je m'adresser pour expédier un message qui doit être répété?*	ah kee dwah-zher madresseh poor expehd'yeh u**n** messahahz kee dwaht^aitr' rehpehteh?
I will connect you with our Service Department — they will attend to same	*Je vais vous mettre en communication avec le département du service*	zher vai voo mettr' ah**n** commeuneecahss'yo**n** avek ler dehpahrt'-mah**n** deu sairveess
What is the time?	*Quelle heure est-il?*	kel^err ait-eel
The time is eight-thirty	*Il est huit heures et demie*	eel'ai eueet^err ai d'mee

English	French	Pronunciation
What is the difference in time between Montreal and France?	Quelle est la différence d'heure entre Montréal et la France?	kel ai lah deefehrahnss dērr ahntr monreh'-ahl ai lah frahnss
Difference in time is five hours forward	La France est en avance de cinq heures sur Montréal	la frahnss ait^ahn^ avahnss der sank^ērr sēur monreh'ahl
What was the final score of last night's hockey game?	Quel fut le résultat final de la joute de "hockey" hier soir?	kel fēu ler rehzēultah feenahl der lah zhoot der hockey yair swahr
The score was three to one in favour of Canadiens	Le résultat final fut de trois à un pour les Canadiens	ler rehzēultah feenahl fēu der twahz^ah un poor lai canahd'yans
Could you give me a report on weather conditions at St. Jovite?	Pouvez-vous me dire quelles sont les conditions atmosphériques à St. Jovite?	pooveh-voo mer deer kel son lai condeess'yon atmosfehreek ah san zhoveet?
St. Jovite reports good weather conditions.	Les conditions atmosphériques sont excellentes à St. Jovite	lai condeess'yon atmosfehreek sont^exsellahn ah san zhoveet
What are your different cable rates to France?	Quels sont les différents taux pour câbler en France?	kel son lai deeffehrahn toh poor cahbleh ahn frahnss
The ordinary rate to France is ... cents per word, code ... cents per word, deferred rate ... cents per word, the night letter of NLT rates ... twenty-five word minimum	Le tarif ordinaire pour la France est ... sous du mot, en code ... sous du mot, le tarif différé ... sous du mot, lettre de nuit ..., minimum de 25 mots	ler tahreef ohrdeenair poor la frahnss ai ... soo dēu moh, ahn cohd ... soo dēu moh, ler tahreef deefehreh ... soo dēu moh, lettr de nēuee ... meeneemum der van-san mohs
Is the prefix chargeable?	Est-ce que le préfixe doit être payé?	ess ker ler prehfeex dwaht ^aitr' paiyeh
Yes, the prefix is chargeable	Oui, il doit être payé	wee, eel dwaht^aitr' pai'-yeh

Italic r and i silent; thick n indicates nasal; apostrophe indicates suppressed vowel.

English	French	Pronunciation
It is a collect message	C'est un message dont les frais doivent être payés par le destinataire.	saitˆun messahzh don lai frai dwahv't'ˆaitr pai'yeh pahr ler daisteenahtair
Do you refuse to pay the charges?	Refusez-vous de payer les frais?	rerfeŭzeh-voo der pai'yeh lai frai?
Confirmation has been mailed to you	La confirmation a été mise à la Poste	la confeermahss'yon ah ehteh meez ah lah post'
There will be no extra charges	Il n'y aura pas de frais supplémentaires	eel nee ohrah pah der frai seŭpplehmahntair
One moment, please	Un instant, s'il vous plaît	ērnˆanstahn, seel voo plai
Messengers will be there momentarily	Le messager sera chez vous d'un moment à l'autre	ler messahzheh s'rah sheh voo dun momahn ah lohtr'
I will look into the case and call you back as soon as possible	Je vais immédiatement m'occuper de la chose et vous rappellerai	zher vaizˆeemmehdeeaht'mahn mockeŭpeh der lah shohz ai voo rappell'reh
Sorry your call-box is out of order	Nous le regrettons, mais votre appareil pour signaler les messagers est en mauvais état	noo ler rergretton, mai votr' apparaiee poor seenyaleh lai messahzhehs aitˆahn mohvaizˆehtah
It will be attended to immediately	Nous allons y voir immédiatement	noozˆallonzˆee vwahr eemehdeeaht'mahn
Messenger is on the way to you	Le messager est parti pour votre bureau	ler messahzheh ai pahr-tee poor votr' beŭroh
Will you please let me speak to the messenger?	Laissez-moi parler au messager	laisseh-mwah pahrleh oh messahzheh
Please pay charges to the messenger	Veuillez payer les frais au messager	vēree'yeh paiyeh lai frai oh messahzheh
I will advise you as soon as call box is in order	Je vais vous aviser aussitôt que votre appareil pour signaler les messagers sera en bon état	zher vai voozˆaveezeh ohsseetoh ker votr' apparaiee poor seen'yaleh lai messahzheh s'rah ahn bonˆ ehtah

---

Italic *r* and *i* silent; thick **n** indicates nasal; apostrophe indicates suppressed vowel.

English	French	Pronunciation
Will you please telephone for a messenger?	*Veuillez téléphoner pour appeler un messager*	vēree'yeh tehlehfoneh poor app'leh un messahzheh
Have you a telegram for —?	*Avez-vous un télégramme pour . . .?*	aveh-vooz'un tehlehgram poor . . .?
What is the number of the telegram?	*Quel est le numéro du télégramme?*	kel ai ler nēumehroh dēu tehlehgram?
What is the messenger's number?	*Quel est le numéro du messager?*	kel ai ler nēumehroh dēu messahzheh
What is the date on the notice?	*Quelle est la date de l'avis?*	kel ai lah dat der lahvee?
What is your address?	*Quelle est votre adresse?*	kel ai votr' adress?
Has the addressee left?	*Est-ce que le destinataire est parti?*	ess ker ler daisteenahtair ai pahrtee
Do you expect him to return?	*Doit-il revenir?*	dwaht-eel rerv'neer?
When?	*Quand?*	kahn?
Can you tell me where the addressee is employed?	*Pouvez-vous me dire où le destinataire est employé?*	pooveh-voo mer deer oo ler daisteenahtair ait ahnplwah'yeh?
Can you give me his new address?	*Pouvez-vous me donner son adresse?*	pooveh-voo mer dunneh son adress
What time do you wish the message delivered?	*A quelle heure désirez-vous que nous fassions la livraison du télégramme?*	ah kel ērr dehzeereh-voo ker noo fass'yon lah leevraizondēu tehlehgram?
Messenger is out with message	*Le messager est parti avec le télégramme*	ler messahzheh ai pahrtee avek ler tehlehgram
What is your telephone number?	*Quel est votre numéro de téléphone?*	kel ai votr' nēumehroh der tehlehfohn?
I will call you back in a few minutes	*Je vous rappellerai dans quelques instants*	zher voo rappell'reh dahn kelk'z'anstahn
I will send it immediately	*Je vais l'envoyer immédiatement*	zher vai lahnvwah'yeh eemmehd'yat'mahn
Are tolls to be charged to your account?	*Doit-on charger les frais à votre compte?*	dwaht-on shahrzheh lai frai ah votr' cont

Italic *r* and *i* silent; thick **n** indicates nasal; apostrophe indicates suppressed vowel.

English	French	Pronunciation
Do you wish message forwarded at full rate or day letter, or as a night letter?	*Désirez-vous que nous fassions l'expédition du télégramme au tarif ordinaire ou à celui de lettre de jour ou lettre de nuit?*	dehzeereh-voo ker noo fahss'yon lexpehdee-s'yon deū tehlehgram, oh tahreef ohrdeenair oo ah serleūee der lettr der zhoor oo lettr der neūee
It will be delivered tomorrow morning	*Il sera délivré demain matin*	eel s'rah dehleevreh d'man matan
Please send a messenger boy to . . .	*Veuillez envoyer un messager à . . . .*	vēree'yeh ahnvwah'yeh un messahzheh ah . . .
Thank you, we will send one immediately	*Merci, nous vous en envoyons un immédiatement*	mairsee, noo vooẑahn̂ ahnvwah'yonẑun eemehdeeat'mahn
I am expecting a message from . . . As I am leaving town please forward to me at . . .	*J'attends un télégramme, et comme je dois quitter la ville, veuillez me le faire parvenir à . . .*	zhattahnẑun tehlehgram ai com zher dwah keeteh lah veel, vēr'yeh mer ler fair pahrv'-neer ah . . .
Please send us some blanks, both telegrams and cables	*Faites-nous parvenir des formules de câblogrammes et de télégrammes, s'il vous plaît*	fait-noo pahrv'neer dai fohrmeūl der cahblogram ai der tehlehgram, seel voo plai
Thank you—we will send them right away	*Merci, nous vous les expédions immédiatement*	mairsee, noo voo laiẑex-pehd'yonẑeemmeh-dyaht'mahn
What are your special greeting rates to . . .?	*Quel est votre tarif de faveur pour messages de souhaits?*	kel ai votr' tahreef der fahvērr poor messahzh der sou'ai
Will my message be delivered on Christmas Day?	*Allez-vous délivrer mon télégramme le jour de Noël?*	alleh-voo dehleevreh mon tehlehgram ler zhoor der noh-el
If you wish it delivered on Christmas Day, we will arrange to	*Oui, si c'est là votre désir, nous en ferons la livraison le jour de Noël*	wee, see sai lah votr' deh-zeer, nooẑahn f'ron lah leevraizon ler zhoor der noh-el

Italic *r* and *i* silent; thick **n** indicates nasal; apostrophe indicates suppressed vowel.

English	French	Pronunciation
How soon can you get a message into Vancouver?	*Quand pouvez-vous transmettre un télégramme à Vancouver*	kahn pooveh-voo trahn-zmettr' un tehlehgram ah vancouver
In a few minutes, we have direct communication to the Coast	*Dans quelques minutes, car nous sommes en relation directe avec Vancouver*	dahn kelker meenêut, cahr noo sumẑahn rerlas'yon deerect avek vancouver
The Manager is out at present; is there anything I can do for you?	*L'Agent est absent, puis-je vous être utile?*	lahzhahntˆaitˆabsahn, pêuee-zher vooz-aitr' êuteel?
Have you a message for . . . .?	*Avez-vous un télégramme pour . . .?*	aveh-voozˆun tehlehgram poor . . .
What is your address and telephone number?	*Quelle est votre adresse et votre numéro de téléphone?*	kel ai votr' adress ai votr' nêumehro der tehlehfohn?
My address is . . . . and 'phone number	*Mon adresse est . . ., et mon téléphone . . . .*	mon adress' ai . . ., ai mon tehlehfohn . . .
Have you received any notice from us?	*Avez-vous reçu notre avis?*	aveh-voo rersêu notr' ahvee
What is the number on the message?	*Quel est le numéro sur le télégramme?*	kel ai ler nêumehroh sêur ler tehlehgram
I want a message repeated	*Je désire que l'on répète le message*	zher dehzeer ker lon rehpait ler messahzh
Will you give me particulars?	*Voulez-vous me donner les détails?*	vooleh-voo mer dunneh lai dehtahee
If a message comes in addressed to me, please forward same to the following address	*Si vous recevez un télégramme pour moi, s'il vous plaît, me le faire parvenir à l'adresse suivante . . .*	see voo rers'vehzˆun tehlehgram poor mwah, seel voo plait mer ler fair pahrv'neer ah ladress sêueevahnt . . .
Do you want your message forwarded, charges prepaid or collect?	*Désirez-vous payer les frais ou doit-on expédier votre télégramme payable sur livraison?*	dehseereh-voo pai'yeh lai frai oo dwaht-on expehdyeh votre tehlehgram pai'yahbl' sêur leevraizon

Italic *r* and *i* silent; thick **n** indicates nasal; apostrophe indicates suppressed vowel.

English	French	Pronunciation
Please have one of your representatives call and see us	*Voudriez-vous envoyer un de vos représentants nous voir?*	voodr'yeh-vooz⌢ahn-vwah'yeh un der voh rerprehzahntahn noo vwahr?
What is the name and address, please?	*Quel est le nom et l'adresse, s'il vous plaît?*	kel ai ler non ai' ladress, seel voo plai?
The name and address are . . .	*Le nom et l'adresse sont . . .*	ler non ai ladress son . . .
We are vacating our present address. We are moving to	*Nous quittons nos bureaux et déménageons à . . .*	noo keetons noh beūroh ai dehmehnazhon ah . . . .
Do you wish us to install a call box? When do you want it installed?	*Désirez-vous que nous installions un appareil d'appel pour messagers? Si oui, quand?*	dehseereh-voo ker nooz⌢anstall'yonz⌢un⌢appahraiee dappel poor messahzheh? see wee, kahn?
Whom do you want your messages telephoned to after hours?	*Où voulez-vous que nous téléphonions vos télégrammes après les heures de bureaux?*	oo vooleh-voo ker noo tehlehfohn'yon voh tehlehgram aprai laiz⌢ērr der beūroh?
You can telephone, etc.	*Vous pouvez téléphoner à . . .*	voo pooveh tehlehfohneh ah . . .
Have you direct communication with?	*Etes-vous en communication directe avec . . .?*	ait-vooz'ahn commeūneecas'yon deerect avek . . . .
What are your connections in the United States?	*Quelles sont vos affiliations américaines?*	kel son vohz⌢affeeleeas'yon amehreecan?
The Postal Telegraph Company	*La Compagnie "Postal Telegraph-Cable Company"*	la conpahnyee "Postal Telegraph-Cable Company

Ships at Sea

I want to send a message to a passenger on a boat	*Je désire expédier un télégramme à un passager en mer*	zher dehzeer expehd'yeh un tehlehgram ah un passahzheh ahn mair

English	French	Pronunciation
When did the boat sail?	*Quand le paquebot est-il parti?*	kah**n** ler pahk'bok a*i*teel pahrtee?
The boat sailed on . . .	*Il est parti le . . .*	eel a*i* pahrtee ler . . .
Where is the boat bound for?	*Quelle est sa destination?*	kel a*i* sa*h* da*i*steenah-s'*i*o**n**?
The boat is due to arrive at Montreal on the afternoon of . . .	*Le paquebot doit arriver à Montréal dans l'après-midi du . . .*	ler pahk'bot dwaht^ar-reeveh ah mo**n**reh-ahl dah**n** lahpra*i*-meedee de**û** . . .
What is the cost per word?	*Quel est le tarif par mot?*	kel a*i* ler tahreef pahr moh
The cost is . . . per word	*Le coût est de . . . du mot*	ler coo a*i* der . . . de**û** moh
Address and signature are charge-able words	*L'adresse et la signature doivent être comptées et payées*	ladress a*i* lah seen'yah-te**û**r dwahvt^a*i*tr con-teh a*i* pa*i*'yeh

In an Express Office

What is the rate from . . . to . . . ?	*Quel est le tarif de . . . à . . . ?*	kel a*i* ler tahreef der . . . ah . . . ?
The rate from . . . to . . . is $ . . . per 100 lbs	*Le tarif, de . . . à . . . est de $ . . . par 100 livres*	ler tahreef, der . . . ah . . . , a*i* der . . . dollahr par sah**n** leevr'
How much will it cost to send a shipment weigh-ing . . . lbs. From . . . to . . . ?	*Combien en coûte-t-il pour expédier un colis pesant . . . livres, de . . . à . . . ?*	conb'ya**n** ahn coot'teel poor expehd'yeh un colee perzah**n** . . . leevr', der . . . ah . . . ?
The charge for . . . lbs. from . . . to . . . is $ . . .	*Il en coute $ . . . pour . . . liv., de . . . à . . .*	eel ah**n** coot . . . dollahr pour . . . leevr', der . . . ah . . .
Is this the minimum charge?	*Est-ce là un prix minimum?*	ess lah un pree mee-neemom?
No, charges are as-sessed according to the weight of the shipment	*Non, les prix sont fixés suivant le poids des colis*	non, la*i* pree so**n** feexeh se**û**eevah**n** ler pwah da*i* colee
How much does the shipment weigh?	*Quel est le poids de cet envoi?*	kel a*i* ler pwah der set ah**n**vwah?

Italic *r* and *i* silent; thick **n** indicates nasal; apostrophe indicates suppressed vowel.

English	French	Pronunciation
The shipment weighs . . . lbs.	L'envoi pèse . . . livres	lah**n**vwah pa*i*z' . . . leevr'
Is there delivery service at . . .?	Y a-t-il un service de livraison à . . .?	yahteel u**n** sairveess de*r* leevra*i*zo**n** ah . . .?
Yes . . . No . . .	Oui . . . Non . . .	Wee . . . no**n** . . .
Does this charge include Insurance?	Le coût d'expédition comprend-il l'assurance	ler coo dexpehdees'yo**n** co**n**prah**n**t-eel lahssēūrah**n**ss?
Yes, provided the shipment is not valued over $50.00 If valued over $50.00 an additional charge is made upon the excess value	Oui, pourvu que la valeur de l'envoi n'excède pas $50.00 Si cette valeur dépasse $50.00, il faut payer un supplément pour l'excédent	wee, poorvēū ke*r* lah vah-lē*r*r de*r* lah**n**vwah nex-sa*i*d' pah sa**n**kah**n**t dollahr. see set vah-lē*r*r dehpahss sa**n**kah**n**t dollahr, eel foh pai'yeh u**n** sēūppleh-mah**n** poor lexseh-dah**n**
If this shipment leaves . . . today, when will it get to . . .?	Si cet envoi est expédié aujourd'hui de . . . , quand arrivera-t-il à . . .?	see set ah**n**vwah a*i*tˆex-pehd'yeh ohzhoor-dēūee de . . . kah**n**tˆ arreev'rah-teel ah . . .?
If shipment leaves on tonight's train, it will reach . . . at . . . o'clock in the morning and should be delivered shortly thereafter	Si l'envoi part par le train de ce soir, il arrivera à . . . , à . . . heures du matin et sera livré peu après	see lah**n**vwah pahr pahr ler tra**n** de*r* se*r* swahr, eel arreev'rah ah . . . ah . . . ērr dēū mata**n** a*i* s'rah leevreh pē*r* ahpra*i*
What is the U.S. Port of Entry for a shipment going to . . .?	Quel est le point d'entrée aux Etats-Unis pour un envoi expédié à . . .?	kel a*i* ler pwa**n** d'ah**n**-treh ohzˆehtahzˆēūnee poor ē**r**n ah**n**vwah ex-pehd'yeh ah . . .
The U.S. Port of Entry for this shipment is . . .	Le point d'entrée aux Etats-Unis pour un tel envoi est . . .	ler pwa**n** d'ah**n**treh ohzˆ-ehtahzˆēūnee poor u**n** tel ah**n**vwah a*i* . . .
How will this shipment be routed?	Par quelle route cet envoi sera-t-il acheminé?	pahr kel root set ah**n**-vwah s'rah-teel ahsh'-meeneh?

Italic *r* and *i* silent; thick **n** indicates nasal; apostrophe indicates suppressed vowel.

English	French	Pronunciation
Where will this shipment be transferred to the . . . Express Company?	*Où cet envoi sera-t-il transféré à la Compagnie de Messageries . . .*	oo set ahnvwah s'rahteel trahnssfehreh ah lah conpanyee der messahzherree . . .?
This shipment will be transferred to the . . . Express Company at . . .	*Cet envoi sera transféré à la Compagnie de Messageries . . . à . . .*	set ahnvwah s'rah trahnssfehreh ah lah conpan'yee der messahzherree ah . . .
How will I route this shipment?	*Comment devrais-je acheminer cet envoi?*	commahn dervrai-zher ahshermeeneh set ahnvwah
This shipment should be routed via . . . and Canadian Pacific Express	*Cet envoi devra être acheminé via . . . et les Messageries du Pacifique Canadien*	set ahnvwah dervrah aitr ahshermeeneh veeah . . . ai lai messahzherree deü pahsseefeek canahd'yan
What papers are required for shipment going to the United States?	*Quels pièces et documents faut-il avoir pour expédier un envoi aux Etats-Unis?*	kel peeaiss ai dokeümahn foht-eel avvwahr poor expehd'yeh ern ahnvwah ohz^ehtahz^ eünee
Shipments for the United States must be accompanied by copy of shipping receipt, invoices in duplicate, Export Entry in duplicate and Consular Certificate if valued over $100.00	*Les envois expédiés aux Etats-Unis doivent être accompagnés d'une copie du reçu d'expédition, des factures en double, de l'entrée d'exportation en double et d'un certificat du consulat, si la valeur s'élève à plus de $100.00*	laiz^ahnvwahz^expehd'yehz^ohz^ehtahz^eünee dwahvt^aitr acconpan'yeh deün copee deü rersseü d'expehdees'yon, dai facteürz^ahn doobl', der la'hntreh dexpohrtahs'yon ahn doobl' ai dun sairteefeecat deü conseülah, see lah vahlērr sehlaiv ah pleü der sahn dollahr
Where is the duty assessed?	*Où les droits de douane sont-ils fixés?*	oo lai drwah der d'wahn sont-eel feexeh?

English	French	Pronunciation
The duty is assessed at the U.S. Port of Entry	*Les droits de douane sont fixés au point d'entrée aux Etats-Unis*	lai drwah der d'wahn son feexeh oh pwan d'ahntreh ohzˆeh-tahzˆeūnee
How is the duty collected?	*Comment les droits de douane sont-ils perçus?*	commahn lai drwah der d'wahn sont-eel pairsēu?
Agent at shipping point can make arrangements for collection of duty, entry fee, etc., from either shipper or consignee, as desired	*L'agent en service au point d'expédition peut faire les arrangements nécessaires pour la perception des droits de douane, droits d'entrée, etc., de l'expéditeur ou du destinataire, suivant le cas*	lazhahn ahn sairveess oh pwan dexpehdee-s'yon pēr fair laizˆar-rahnzh'mahn nehsessair poor lah pairsep-s'yon dai drwah der d'wahn, drwah dahn-treh, ehtsehterah, der l'expehdeetērr oo dēu daisteenatair, sēuee-vahn ler cah
Can I send this shipment charges collect?	*Puis-je expédier cet envoi en faisant payer les frais de transport par le destinataire?*	pēuee-zher expehd'yeh set ahnvwah ahn ferzahn pai'yeh lai frai der trahnspohr pahr ler daisteenatair?
Yes, express charges can be collected from consignee if desired	*Oui, les frais de transport peuvent être payés par le destinataire, si l'on veut*	wee, lai frai der trahns-pohr pērvtˆaitr' pai'yeh pahr ler daisteena-tair, see lon vēr
A shipment was forwarded from . . . to . . . on (date) and has not yet been received. This is urgently required and our factory is tied up. What can you do to locate it?	*Un envoi a été expédié de . . . à . . . le (date) et n'a pas encore été reçu. Pouvez-vous le retracer? Nous en avons un besoin urgent à notre usine*	un ahnvwah ah ehteh expehd'yeh der . . . ah . . . ler (dat) eh nah pahzˆahncohr ehteh rersēu pooveh-voo ler rertrasseh? noozˆahn avonzˆun berzwan ēurzhahn ah notr' ēuzeen

---

Italic *r* and *i* silent; thick **n** indicates nasal; apostrophe indicates suppressed vowel.

English	French	Pronunciation
We shall be glad to trace the shipment by telegraph. Please let me have shipper's and consignee's names. We would also like to know what the shipment consisted of and the approximate weight	*Nous ferons notre possible pour le retracer par télégraphe. Veuillez nous donner les noms de l'expéditeur et du destinataire. Il nous faudrait aussi savoir en quoi consiste l'envoi et quel en est le poids approximatif*	noo f'ron notr' posseebl' poor ler rertrasseh pahr tehlehgraf. vēree'yeh noo dunneh lai non der lexpehdeetērr eh dēu daisteenatair. eel noo fohdrai ohssi sahvwahr ahn kwah conseest' lahnvwa eh kel ahn ai ler pwah approxeemahteef
When can we expect a reply?	*Pourrez-vous nous donner une réponse bientôt?*	pourreh-voo noo donneh ēun rehponss b'yantoh?
We expect a reply later on this afternoon or the first thing in the morning, and will give you a call immediately	*Nous attendons une réponse plus tard cet après-midi ou de bonne heure demain matin. Nous vous appellerons dès que nous l'aurons reçue*	noozˆattahndonzˆēun rehpons plēu tahr setˆahprai-meedee oo der bunnˆērr derman mahtan. noo voozˆapp'leron dai ker noo lohron rersēu
Shipment was forwarded from . . . to . . . in error. Will you have your agent at . . . reforward it to . . ?	*L'envoi a été expédié de . . . à . . . par erreur. Voulez-vous demander à votre agent de . . ., de le réexpédier à . . . ?*	lahnvwah ah ehteh expehd'yeh der . . . ah . . . pahr airērr. vooleh-voo d'mahndeh ah notr' ahzhahn der . . . der ler reh-expehd'yeh à . . .

Italic *r* and *i* silent; thick **n** indicates nasal; apostrophe indicates suppressed vowel.

English	French	Pronunciation
Yes, we will write our agent tonight to re-forward this shipment to .. but it will be necessary for you to send us a letter authorizing us to re-address the shipment. Will you send this letter to us tonight?	*Oui, nous écrirons ce soir à notre agent, lui demandant de réexpédier l'envoi à . . . , mais vous devrez nous adresser une lettre nous autorisant à ré-adresser cet envoi. Voulez-vous nous envoyer cette lettre, ce soir?*	wee, nooz̑ehcreeron ser swahr ah notr ahzh-ahn, lêûee d'mahn-dahn der reh-expeh-d'yeh l'ahnvwa à . . ., mai voo dervreh nooz̑ ahdresseh êûn lettr' nooz̑ohtoreezahn ah reh-ahdresseh set̑ ahnvwah. vooleh-voo nooz̑ahnvwahyeh set' lettr, ser swar?
We have a shipment of films coming in Sunday morning. Can we send this out on train No. ... to ... so it will be there for the afternoon show?	*Nous attendons un envoi de pellicules cinématographiques dimanche ma-tin. Pouvons-nous l'expédier à . . . par le train No. . . ., afin qu'il ar-rive à destination à temps pour la re-présentation de l'après-midi?*	nooz̑attahndonz̑ern̑ ahnvwa der pelleekêûl seenehmahtografeek deemahnsh mahtan poovon-noo lexpeh-d'yeh ah . . . pahr ler tran nêûmehroh . . . ahfan keel arreev ah daisteenas'yon poor lah rerprehzahntah-s'yon der l'ahprai-meedee?
We have no service on this train on Sunday, but in this particular case, will be glad to help you out, and will issue the necessary instruc-tions. It will be necessary for your man to take de-livery of this ship-ment Sunday morning and re-address it	*Nous n'avons pas de service de messa-geries par ce train, le dimanche, mais pour vous aider dans ce cas-ci, je donnerai les in-structions néces-saires. Votre em-ployé devra prendre livraison de cet en-voi dimanche ma-tin et voir à le réadresser*	noo navon pah der sair-veess der messahzh'ree pahr ser tran, ler dee-mahnsh, mai poor vooz̑aideh dahn ser cah-see, zher donn'reh laiz̑anstrêûcs'yon nehsessair. votr' ahn-plwah'yeh dervrah prahndr' leevraizon der set̑ahnvwah dee-mahnsh matan ai vwahr ah ler rehadres-seh

---

Italic *r* and *i* silent; thick n indicates nasal; apostrophe indicates suppressed vowel.

English	French	Pronunciation
What is the nearest station to . . .?	*Quelle est la gare la plus proche de . . .?*	kel a*i* lah gahr lah pléû prosh de*r* . . .?
The nearest station to . . . is . . . ?	*La gare la plus proche de . . . est . . .*	la gahr lah pléû prosh de*r* . . . a*i* . . .
Will this shipment (live stock or animals) be properly looked after and fed and watered?	*Ces bêtes seront-elles nourries et abreuvées convenablement au cours du voyage?*	sa*i* ba*i*t s'ro**n**t-ell nooree a*i* abrérveh con**v**'-nahbl' mah**n** oh coor déû vwah'yahzh?
Yes, our Messenger on the train will look after the animals and feed and water them according to directions. The necessary food and utensils, of course, must be supplied by the shipper	*Oui, notre messager à bord du train prendra soin de ces bêtes, leur donnera à manger et à boire conformément aux instructions. Naturellement, l'expéditeur doit fournir la nourriture et les ustensiles nécessaires*	wee, notr' messahzheh ah bohr déû tra**n** prahndrah swa**n** de*r* sa*i* bait, lé*r*r donn'rah ah mah**n**zheh a*i* ah bwahr confohrmehmah**n** ohz^anstréûc'syo**n**. natéûrell'mah**n**, l'expehdeetè*r*r dwah foorneer la nooreetéû*r* a*i* laiz^anstréûcs'yo**n** nehsessa*i*r
This shipment is very fragile. Will it be carefully handled?	*Cet envoi est très fragile. Sera-t-il manié avec précaution?*	set^ah**n**vwah a*i* tra*i* frahzheel. s'rah-teel mahn'yeh avek prehcohs'yo**n**?
Yes, it will be properly labelled and given special attention all along the line	*Oui, il sera étiqueté comme il convient et sera l'objet d'une attention toute spéciale sur tout le parcours*	wee, eel s'rah ehteek'teh com eel con**v**'ya**n** a*i* s'rah lobzha*i* déû**n** attah**n**s'yo**n** toot spehs'yahl séû*r* too le*r* pahrcoor
Is there any danger of this perishable shipment being exposed to excessive cold or heat?	*Y a-t-il danger que cet envoi de marchandises périssables soit exposé à un froid excessif ou à une chaleur trop vive?*	yahteel dah**n**zheh ke*r* set^ah**n**vwah de*r* marshah**n**deez pehreessahbl swaht expohseh ah u**n** frwaht^exsesseev oo ah éû**n** shahlè*r*r troh veev

English	French	Pronunciation
No, this shipment will be properly labelled and employees handling it will see that it is protected from extreme cold and kept away from steam pipes	*Non, cet envoi sera étiqueté comme il convient et les employés qui auront à s'en occuper verront à ce qu'il ne soit pas placé près des radiateurs, ni exposé à un trop grand froid*	non, set^ahnvwah s'rah ehteekteh com eel conv'yan et laiz^ahn plwah'yeh kee ohront ah sahn^ockeûpeh vairront ah ser keel ner swah pah plahsseh prai dai rad'yahtērr, nee expohzeh ah un troh grahn frwah
Ship by Canadian Pacific Express	*Expédiez par Messageries du Pacifique Canadien*	expehd'yeh pahr messahzh'ree deû pahsseefeek canahd'yan
All shipments, large or small, receive prompt attention and careful handling	*Tous les envois, sans égard à leur importance, sont l'objet d'une attention immédiate et sont maniés avec précaution*	too laiz^ahnvwah, sahnz ^ehgahr ah lērr anpohrtahnss, son lobzhai deûn attahns'yon eemmehd'yat ai son mahn'yeh avek prehcohs'yon
Express charges may be prepaid or collected at destination, unless shipment is destined to a point where there is no Agent	*Les frais de transport par messageries sont payés à l'avance ou recouvrés à destination, à moins que l'envoi soit fait à un endroit où il n'y a pas d'agent*	lai frai der trahnspohr pahr messazh'ree son paiyeh ah lavahnss oo rercoovrehz ah daisteenahs'yon, ah mwan ker lahnvwah swah fai ah ērn^ahndrwah oo eel nyah pah dahzhahn
What is the charge per 100 lbs. to Quebec City?	*Quel est le tarif par 100 livres pour expédition à Québec?*	kel ai ler tahreef pahr sahn leeve poor expehdees'yon ah kehbec
What time does train leave and from what station?	*A quelle heure le train part-il et de quelle gare?*	ah kel ērr ler tran pahrt-eel ai der kel gahr
Have you received a box, parcel, etc., addressed to . . .?	*Avez-vous reçu une boîte, un colis, etc., adressé à . . . ?*	aveh-voo rersseû eûn bwaht, un colee, etc., ahdresseh ah

Italic *r* and *i* silent; thick **n** indicates nasal; apostrophe indicates suppressed vowel.

English	French	Pronunciation
What is your street address, Sir or Madam?	*Quelle est votre adresse, Monsieur ou Madame?*	kel a*i* vot*r'* ahdress, mer-s'yē*r* oo madahm?
What does parcel contain?	*Que renferme le colis?*	ker rahn*f*airm le*r* colee
Where is it from?	*D'où vient-il?*	doo v'ya*n*t-eel?
What is the value?	*Quelle est la valeur?*	kel a*i* lah vahlē*r*r
When was it shipped?	*Quant fut-il expédié?*	kahn feūt-eel expehd'yeh
What is your name?	*Quel est votre nom?*	kel a*i* vot*r* non
Hold the line please	*Restez à l'appareil, s'il vous plaît*	restehz̄ah l'appahra*i*ee, seel voo pla*i*
Is the trunk being checked on your ticket?	*La malle est-elle enregistrée avec votre billet?*	lah mahl a*i*t-ell ahnrer-zheestreh avek votr' bee'ya*i*?
Sorry, we do not pick up baggage moving on your ticket, please call the Transfer Company or local carter	*Nous le regrettons, mais nous ne faisons pas l'enlèvement des bagages devant être enregistrés avec les billets. Veuillez vous adresser à un charretier ou à une entreprise de camionnage*	noo le*r* rergretton, ma*i* noo ne*r* ferzon pah l'ahnla*i*v'mahn da*i* bagazh dervahnt'a*i*tr ahnrezheestreh avek la*i* bee'yai. vē*r*'yeh vooz̄adresseh ah un sharr't'yeh oo ah eūn ahntr̄preez der cam'-yonnazh
Will you please call train Inquiry?	*Appelez, s'il vous plaît, le service de renseignements concernant les trains*	app'leh, seel voo pla*i*, ler sa*i*rvee*s*s der rahn-sa*i*n'yermahn con-sa*i*rnahn la*i* tran
We do not perform local cartage	*Nous ne faisons pas de camionnage*	noo ne*r* ferzon pah le*r* cam'yonnazh
One moment, please	*Un instant, s'il vous plaît*	ē*r*n̄anstan, seel voo pla*i*
Do you wish to pre-pay the charges?	*Désirez-vous payer les frais à l'avance?*	dehz̄ereh-voo pa*i*'yeh la*i* fra*i* ah lahvahnss?
The charge is . . .	*Les frais s'élèvent à . . .*	la*i* fra*i* sehla*i*v' ah . . .

Italic *r* and *i* silent; thick **n** indicates nasal; apostrophe indicates suppressed vowel.

English	French	Pronunciation
The train leaves at ..	*Le train part à . . .*	le*r* tra**n** pahrt ah . . .
The train arrives at ..	*Le train arrive à . . .*	le*r* tra**n** arreev' ah . . .
This being a legal holiday we have no pick-up service and we are delivering perishable traffic only	*Comme c'est jour de fête, nous n'avons pas de service d'enlèvement et nous ne faisons la livraison que des envois de nature périssable*	com sa*i* zhoor de*r* fa*i*t, noo nahvo**n** pah de*r* sairveess dahn la*i*v'-mahn a*i* noo ne*r* ferso**n** lah leevra*i*zo**n** ke*r* da*i*zˆahnvwah de*r* nahteūr pehreessahbl'
The Wagon Service Department is closed — may we take your call for tomorrow?	*Le service de camionnage est interrompu — voulez-vous que nous inscrivions votre appel pour demain?*	le*r* sairveess de*r* cam'-yonnazh a*i*tˆan tairronpeū — vooleh-voo ke*r* noozˆanscreev' yo**n** votr' appel poor d'ma**n**
Our Depot Office is always open	*Notre bureau de dépôt est toujours ouvert*	notr' beūroh de*r* dehpoh a*i* toozhoorzˆoova*i*r
We do not pick up or deliver on Sunday	*Nous ne faisons pas la livraison ni l'enlèvement des colis à domicile le dimanche*	noo ne*r* ferzo**n** pah lah leevra*i*zo**n** nee lahn la*i*v'mahn da*i* colee ah domeesseel le*r* dee-mahnsh
If you pick up a shipment at my house, will the charges be any more than if I bring it to your office?	*Si vous venez chercher un colis chez moi, les frais seront-ils plus élevés que si je l'apportais moi-même à vos bureaux?*	see voo ve*r*neh shairsheh un colee sheh mwah, la*i* fra*i* s'ront'eel pleūz ˆehl'veh ke*r* see zhe*r* lappohrta*i* mwah-ma*i*m ah voh beūroh
No, we do not charge anything extra for pick-up and delivery	*Non, nous n'exigeons pas de supplément pour la livraison et l'enlèvement des colis*	no**n**, noo negzeezho**n** pah de*r* seūpplehmah**n** poor lah leevra*i*zo**n** a*i* lahn la*i*v'mahn da*i* colee
I received a shipment this morning which is damaged	*J'ai reçu ce matin un envoi qui était endommagé*	zheh re*r*sseū se*r* mahta**n** ērnˆahnvwah kee eh-ta*i* ahndommahzheh
Where was the shipment from?	*D'où venait cet envoi?*	doo ve*r*na*i* setˆahnvwah?

Italic *r* and *i* silent; thick **n** indicates nasal; apostrophe indicates suppressed vowel.

English	French	Pronunciation
Thank you for phoning, we will have an Inspector call on you at once	*Je vous remercie pour avoir téléphoné. J'enverrai un inspecteur vous voir immédiatement*	zher voo reimairsee poor^ avwahr tehlehfohneh. zhahnrairreh ērn^anspectērr voo vwahr eemmehd'yaht'mahn
How do your rates compare with the Post Office?	*Comment vos tarifs se comparent-ils avec ceux de la Poste?*	commahn voh tahreef ser conpahr'teel avek sēr der lah post?
Thank you, we will have an Inspector call on you and explain our small package rates	*Merci, un de nos inspecteurs passera vous voir et vous fera connaître nos tarifs pour l'expédition des petits colis*	mairsee—un der nohz^ anspectērr pahss'rah voo vwahr et voo f'rah connaîtr noh tahreef poor lexpehdees'yon dai p'tee colee
Will you please call for a parcel at 5.30 p.m.?	*Voulez-vous envoyer chercher un colis à 5 h. 30 p.m.?*	vooleh-vooz ahnvwah'-yeh shairsheh un colee ah sank ērr trahnt pai emm?
I am sorry, but our pick-up service closes at 5 p.m.	*Je le regrette, mais notre service d'enlèvement cesse à 5 h. p.m.*	zher ler rergrett, mai notr' sairveess d'ahnlaiv'mahn sess ah sank ērr pai emm
Can I bring the parcel to your depot myself?	*Puis-je alors porter moi-même le colis à votre bureau?*	pŭeezh^ahlohr pohrteh mwah-maim ler colee ah votr bĕuroh
Yes, we will be pleased to accept it from you at the depot	*Oui, nous serons heureux de l'accepter si vous l'apportez*	wee, noo s'ronz ērrēr der lacsepteh see voo lappohrteh
If I make a shipment to Vancouver tonight, when will it arrive there?	*Si je fais un envoi à Vancouver ce soir, quand arrivera-t-il dans cette ville?*	see zher faiz ern^ahnvwah ah vancoover ser swahr, kahnt^arreev'-rah-teel dahn set veel?
On the . . . day at 9.00 a.m.	*Le . . . ème jour, à 9 h. a.m.*	ler . . . aim zhoor, ah nērv^ērr ah emm
Will it be delivered the same day?	*Sera-t-il livré le même jour?*	s'rah-teel leevreh ler maim zhoor?
Yes	*Oui*	wee
I have a shipment for the 4 p.m. train	*J'ai un envoi pour le train de 4 h. p.m.*	zheh ērn^ahnvwah poor ler tran der katr ērr pai emm

---

Italic *r* and *i* silent; thick **n** indicates nasal apostrophe indicates suppressed vowel.

English	French	Pronunciation
I am sorry we could not make that train for you as the train leaves in 20 minutes	*Je le regrette, mais cet envoi ne pourra pas partir par ce train, car celui-ci quittera la gare dans 20 minutes*	zher ler rergrett, mai set^ ahnvwah ner poorrah pah pahrteer pahr ser tran, cahr serleûee-see keet'rah lah gahr dahn van meenêut
If I bring it to the depot myself, will it make the train?	*Si je l'apporte moi-même, pourra-t-il être mis à bord du train?*	see zher l'appohrt mwah-maim, poorrah-teel aitr meez^ah bohr dêu tran
Yes, if you get here 5 minutes before departure of the train	*Oui, si vous arrivez ici 5 minutes avant le départ du train*	wee, see vooz^arreevehz^ eessee san meeneut ahvahn ler dehpahr dêu tran
Until what time may I bring shipments to your Depot?	*Jusqu'a quelle heure puis-je apporter moi-même des colis à vos bureaux*	zhêuskah kel êrr pêueezh ^appohrteh mwah-maim dai colee ah voh bêuroh?
Our Depot office is never closed	*Nos bureaux ne sont jamais fermés*	noh beuroh ner son zha-mai fairmeh
Will you please call for a parcel at ..?	*Voulez-vous faire prendre un colis à ...?*	vooleh-voo fair prahndr' un colee ah ...?
I am sorry Madam, but you are out of our limits. We only go as far as ... If you bring your parcel to the grocer who is in our limits, we will call there for it	*Je le regrette, Madame, mais vous habitez en dehors des limites de notre circuit. Nous allons seulement jusqu'à ... Si vous voulez vous donner le peine de porter votre colis chez l'épicier ... qui se trouve en dedans de ces limites, nous passerons le prendre là*	zher ler rergrett, ma-dahm, mai vooz-abee-teh ahn derhohr dai leemeet der notr seer-kêuee. nooz^allon sêrl'mahn zhêuskah .. see voo vooleh voo donneh lah pain der pohrteh votr colee sheh lehpeess'yeh ... kee ser troov ahn derdahn der sai leemeet, noo pass'ron ler prahndre lah

Expressions in Sale of Financial Paper

English	French	Pronunciation
I wish to purchase a Money Order	*Je voudrais acheter un mandat-express*	zher voodraiz^ahzh'teh un mahn dah-express
Thank you	*Merci*	mairsee
What is the amount?	*Pour quel montant?*	poor kel montahn?
To whom payable?	*A qui doit-il être payé?*	ah kee dwaht-eel aitr' pai'yeh'
Where is the payee located?	*Où habite le bénéficiaire?*	oo abeet ler behnehfeess-s'yair
What is the name of the remitter?	*Quel est le nom de l'envoyeur?*	kel ai ler non der l'ahn-vwahyērr
The amount of the Money Order is . .	*Le montant du mandat-express est de . . .*	ler montahn dēū mahn-dah-express ai der . . .
The Money Order Charge is . . .	*Les frais du mandat-express s'élèvent à . . .*	lai frai dēū mahndah-express sehlaiv ah . . .
The Excise Stamp is . . .	*Le timbre d'accise est de . . .*	ler tanbr' dacseez ai der . . .
Total of . . . please . . .	*Le tout se chiffre à . . .*	ler too ser sheeffr' ah . . .
This is your receipt which should be kept and if the Money Order is lost or stolen just bring the receipt to us and we will issue another Money Order without charge	*Voici votre reçu. Gardez-le, car si le mandat-express venait à être perdu ou volé, vous n'auriez qu'à nous apporter ce reçu et nous vous donnerions un autre mandat sans aucuns frais*	vwahssee votr rerssēū. gahrdeh-ler, cahr see ler mahndah-express v'nait^ah aitr' pairdēū oo voleh, voo n'ohr'yez kah nooz^appohrteh ser rerssēū ai noo voo donn'ryon ērn^ohtre mahndah sahnz^oh-kun frai
The premium (discount) to-day on Money Orders payable in United States Dollars is . . . %	*L'escompte aujourd'hui sur les mandats-express payables en dollars américains est de . . . %*	lescont ohzhoordēūee sēūr lai mahndahj-express pai'yahbl' ahn dollahr amehreecan ai der . . . poor sahn

English	French	Pronunciation
There is no premium or discount on United States Dollar Money Orders to-day	*Il n'y a pas d'escompte aujourd'hui sur les mandats-express payables en dollars américains*	eel n'yah pah descont ohzhoordéuee séur la*i* mah**n**dah-express pai-'yahbl' ah**n** dollahr amehreeca**n**
Will you accept United States Currency in payment of Money Orders (Travellers Cheques) payable in United States Dollars?	*Puis-je acheter, avec de l'argent américain, des mandats-express (chèques de voyageurs) payables en dollars américains?*	péueezh' ahsh'teh, avek de*r* lahrzhah**n**t^amehreeca**n**, da*i* mah**n**dah-express (sha*i*k de*r* vwah'yah zhē*r*r) pa*i*'yabl' ah**n** dollah*r* amehreeca**n**?
Yes, we accept Currency — but not silver—in payment of Money Orders (Travellers Cheques) payable in United States Dollars	*Oui, nous acceptons les billets de banque — mais non les pièces d'argent — en paiement des mandats-express (chèques de voyageurs) payables en dollars américains*	wee nooz^aksepto**n** la*i* bee'yai de*r* bah**n**k — ma*i* no**n** la*i* peea*i*ss' dahrzhah**n**—ah**n** pa*i*mah**n** da*i* mah**n**dah-express (sha*i*k de*r* vwah'yahzhē*r*r) pa*i*y-ahbl ah**n** dollahr amehreeca**n**
I am going abroad and would like some Travellers Cheques	*Je dois partir pour l'étranger et je désire me procurer des chèques de voyageurs*	zher dwah pahrteer poor lehtrah**n**zheh eh zher dehzeer mer prokéureh da*i* sha*i*k de*r* vwah'-yahzhē*r*r
We issue travellers cheques in Canadian and United States Dollars in denominations of $10, $20, $50, and $100, and Sterling in denominations of £2, £5, £10 and £20	*Nous délivrons des chèques de voyageurs en dollars canadiens et américains en coupures de $10, $20, $50 et $100 et en livres sterling en coupures de £2, £5, £10 et £20*	noo dehleevro**n** da*i* sha*i*k der vwah'yahzhē*r*rah**n** dollahr canahd'yan a*i* amehreeca**n**, ah**n** coopéu*r* de*r* dee dollah*r*, va**n**, sa**n**kah**n**t, a*i* sah**n**, a*i* ah**n** leevr stairla**n** ah**n** coopéur der dē*r* leevr', sa**n**k, deess, a*i* va**n**

Italic *r* and *i* silent; thick **n** indicates nasal; apostrophe indicates suppressed vowel.

English	French	Pronunciation
May I ask what countries you intend to visit?	*Puis-je vous demander quels pays vous comptez visiter?*	pêueezh voo d'mahndeh kel paiee voo conteh veezeeteh?
Great Britain, France, and probably some other Continental countries	*La Grande-Bretagne, la Frence et probablement quelques autres pays de l'Europe continentale*	lah grahnd-brertahn'yer, lah frahnss ai probahbl'mahn kelk'zohtr paiee der lērrop conteenahntahl
For Great Britain and Ireland and the Irish Free State, Sterling Travellers Cheques are the best, the United States Dollars next. For Continental countries Sterling or United States Dollar Travellers Cheque are equally good	*Pour la Grande-Bretagne, l'Irlande et l'Etat libre d'Irlande, il vaut mieux avoir des chèques de voyageurs en livres sterling. Pour les pays de l'Europe continentale, les chèques de voyageurs en livres sterling ou en dollars américains sont également recommandables*	poor lah grahnd-brertan'yer, leerlahnd ai lehtahleebr deerlahnd, eel voh m'yēr avwahr dai shaik der vwah'yahzhērr ahn leevr' stairlan poor lai paiee der lērrop conteenahntahl, lai shaik der vwahyahzhērr ahn leevr' stairlan oo ahn dollahr amehreecan sont̂ehgahl'mahn recommahndahbl'
Must I go to a Bank to cash your Travellers Cheques?	*Dois-je me présenter à une banque pour encaisser un de vos chèques de voyageurs?*	dwahzher mer prehzahnteh ah êun bahnk poor ahncaisseh un der voh shaik der vwahyahzhērr?

English	French	Pronunciation
No, you can spend them like money —in hotels, shops, railway, steamship, tourist and express offices, on steamships, in gasoline stations, etc., wherever you happen to be — you may also cash them in thousands of banks the world over. Your own signature is the only identification you require	Non, vous pouvez vous servir de ces chèques comme si c'était de l'argent —dans les hôtels, les magasins, les bureaux de chemins de fer, de bateaux, de tourisme et de messageries, à bord des bateaux, aux postes d'essence, etc., en n'importe quel endroit où vous irez. Vous pouvez aussi les encaisser dans des milliers de banques, dans toutes les parties du monde. Votre signature est la seule identification nécessaire	non, voo pooveh voo sairveer der sai shaik comme see sehtai der lahrzhahn—dahn lai zohtel, lai magahzan lai beûroh der sh'man der fair, der bahtoh, der tooreesm ai der messazh'ree, ah bohr dai bahtoh, oh post' dessahnss, etc., ahn nanpohrt kel ahn-drwah oo vooz'eereh. voo poovehzˆohssee laiz'ahncaisseh dahn dai meel'yeh der bahnk, dahn toot' lai partee deû mond. votr' seen'yateûr ai lah sêrl eedahnteefee-cahs'yon nehsessair
Suppose I lost my Travellers' Cheques?	Et si je perdais mes chèques de voyageurs?	ai see zher pairdai mai shaik de vwahyah-zhêrr?
So long as you have not countersigned the cheques you are protected against loss	Pourvu que les chèques ne soient pas contresignés, vous êtes protégé contre toute perte	poorveû ke lai shaik ner swah pah contr'seen'-yeh, voozˆait proteh-zheh contr toot pairt
How much do they cost?	Combien coûtent-ils?	conb'yan coot-teel?

Italic *r* and *i* silent; thick **n** indicates nasal; apostrophe indicates suppressed vowel.

English	French	Pronunciation

United States Dollar and Sterling Travellers' Cheques cost 75c. per $100. Canadian Dollar Travellers Cheque cost 50c. per $100. They are put up in a neat wallet and are convenient to carry. In addition to Money Orders and Traveller's Cheques we issue Foreign Cheques, transfer money by cable and buy and sell Foreign money

Les chèques de voyageurs en dollars américains et en livres sterling coûtent 75c. par $100, tandis que les chèques en dollars canadiens coûtent seulement 50c. par $100. Ces chèques sont réunis dans un joli portefeuille et se portent commodément sur la personne. En plus des mandats-express et des chèques de voyageurs, nous délivrons des chèques étrangers, envoyons de l'argent par câble et achetons et vendons de l'argent étranger

lai sha*i*k de*r* vwahyah-zhērr ah**n** dollahr amehreecan ai ah**n** leevr stai*r*lan coot' swahssah**n**t-kanz soo pahr sahn dollahr, tahndee ke*r* lai sha*i*k ah**n** dollahr canah-d'yan coot' sē*r*l'mahn sankah**n**t soo pahr sah**n** dollahr. Sa*i* sha*i*k son reh-eūnee dah**n** z'êūn zholee pohrt'fēreeai se*r*pohrt' commohdehmah**n** sēūrlahpai*r*sonn. ah**n** plēū da*i* mahndah-express a*i* da*i* sha*i*k de*r* vwahyahzhērr, noo dehleevro**n** da*i* sha*i*k ehtrah**n**zheh, ah**n**-vwah'yo**n** de*r* lahrzhah**n** pahr cahbl a*i* ash'to**n** a*i* vah**n**don de*r* lahrzhah**n** eh-trah**n**zheh

Ocean Travel

I desire a passage for Paris. (for London—for Brussels)

Je désire un passage pour Paris. (pour Londres — pour Bruxelles)

zher dehzeer **un** passahzh poor Paree (poor Londr' — poor Brēūssell)

By what steamer, on what date, and in what class?

Quel paquebot, à quelle date et en quelle classe?

kell pak'boh, ah kell datt a*i* ah**n** kell clahss?

By the Empress of Britain, sailing June 26th, in Cabin Class (Tourist or Third)

Par l'Empress of Britain, départ du 26 juin, en classe Cabine (classe Touriste ou Troisième)

pahr l'Empress of Britain, dehpahr dēū van-seess zhēūan ah**n** clahss cabeen (clahss tooreest oo trwah'ya*i*m

*Italic r and i silent; thick **n** indicates nasal; apostrophe indicates suppressed vowel.*

English	French	Pronunciation
Where will you disembark, at Cherbourg? at Southampton?	*Où débarquerez-vous? à Cherbourg, ou Southampton?*	oo dehbahrk'reh-voo? ah shairboor oo southampton?
Do you want a room with private bath? or a suite?	*Désirez-vous une chambre avec bain privé, ou une suite?*	dehzeereh-vooz êun shahnbr' avaik ban preeveh, oo êun sêueet?
I desire a reservation at the minimum rate; what can you offer?	*Je désire une place à prix minimum; que pouvez-vous m'offrir?*	zher dehzeer êun plahss ah pree meeneemum; ker pooveh-voo m'offreer?
Room 302 with private bath or 309 without	*Chambre 302 avec bain privé ou 309, sans bain*	shahnbr' trwah sahn dēr ahvek ban preeveh oo trwah sahn nērf, sahn ban
At what price?	*A quel prix?*	ah kell pree?
$250.00 for the one and $220.00 for the other	*Deux cent cinquante dollars pour l'une et deux cent vingt dollars pour l'autre*	dēr sahn sankahnt' dollar poor lun ai dēr sahn van dollar poor lohtr'
Will there be any advantage in taking a round trip passage?	*Y aura-t-il un avantage à prendre un passage aller et retour?*	ee ohrah-t-eel^un^ahvahntahzh^ah prahndr^un pahssahzh alleh ai r'toor?
There is a double advantage; a reduction and in addition a definite reservation for the return trip	*Il y a double avantage: une réduction et en plus une place retenue définitivement pour le retour*	eel^yah doobl^ahvah n tahzh: êun rehdêuks'yon, ai ahn plêu êun plahss rert'nêu dehfeeneeteev'mahn poor ler rertoor
What is the limit of a return ticket, in tourist class or in third class?	*Quelle est la limite de validité du billet de retour, en classe touriste ou en troisième classe?*	kell^ai lah leemeet der valeedeeteh dêu bee'yai der r'toor, ahn klahss tooreest' oo ahn trwahzyaim klahss?
Two years from the date of issue	*Deux ans à compter de la date d'émission*	dērz^ahn ah conteh der lah datt' dehmees-s'yon

---

Italic *r* and *i* silent; thick **n** indicates nasal; apostrophe indicates suppressed vowel.

English	French	Pronunciation
Do you hold a valid passport?	*Avez-vous un passe-port encore valide?*	ahveh-vooz^un pahss-pohr ahn cohr vahleed?
No, I have not got one	*Non, je n'en ai pas*	non, zher nahn^ai pah
or	*(ou)*	(oo)
Yes, it does not expire for two years	*Oui, il n'expire que dans deux ans*	wee, eel nexpeer ker dahn dērz^ahn
or	*(ou)*	(oo)
Yes, but it must be renewed	*Ou, mais il me faut le faire renouveler*	wee, maiz^eel mer foh ler fair rernoov'leh
Here is the necessary application form. Complete and have it signed by a voucher who is one of the persons mentioned in the margin. Return it to me with the photographs and I will secure the passport	*Voici la formule de demande nécessaire. Complétez-la et faites-le signer par un répondant, qui doit être une des personnes mentionnées en marge. Retournez-moi cette formule avec les photographies et j'obtiendrai le passe-port*	vwahssee lah fohrmeûl der d'mahnd' nehses-sair. conplehteh-lah ai fait-lah seenyeh pahr^un rehpondahn, kee dwaht^aitr^eûn deh pairsun' mahns-yoneh ahn mahrzh. Rertoorneh-mwah set fohrmeûl ahvek lai fotograhfee ai zhobt-yandreh ler pahsspohr

When Embarking

English	French	Pronunciation
Your ticket, please	*Votre billet, s'il vous plaît*	votr' bee'yeh, seel voo plai
Here it is	*Le voici*	ler vwahssee
Has my baggage been placed in my cabin?	*Mes bagages seront-ils placés dans ma cabine?*	meh bagahzh' s'ront-eel plahsseh dahn mah cabeen?
Yes, you will find it there	*Oui, vous les y trouverez*	wee, voo laiz^ee troov'-reh
May my friends go on board with me?	*Mes amis peuvent-ils monter à bord avec moi?*	maiz^ahmee pērv't-eel monteh ah bohr avek mwah?

Italic *r* and *i* silent; thick **n** indicates nasal; apostrophe indicates suppressed vowel.

English	French	Pronunciation
Yes, but kindly remind them to leave as soon as the warning to go on shore is sounded	Oui, mais ayez soin de les avertir de quitter le paquebot aussitôt que le clairon sonnera le départ	wee, maiz'ehyeh swan der laiẑahvairteer der keeteh ler pak'boh ohsseetoh ker ler clairon sunn'rah ler dehpahr

On Board Ship

What is the number of your room?	Quelle est le numéro de votre chambre?	kellˆai ler neūmehro der votr' shahnbr'?
129	Cent vingt-neuf	sahn van nērf
Follow me, if you please	Suivez-moi, s'il vous plaît	seūveh-mwah, seel voo plai
Here is the room. The bath-room is there. Here is the electric-bell	Voici la chambre. La salle de bain est là. Voici la sonnette électrique	vwahssee lah shahnbr'. lah sahl der ban ai lah. vwahssee lah sunnait ehlectreek
You may reserve your seat in the Dining Saloon by applying to the Chief Steward in the Dining Saloon. For your deck chair see the Deck Steward. Your room steward will look after the preparing of your bath at the time convenient to you	Vous pourrez retenir votre place à table en vous adressant au maître d'hôtel dans la salle à manger. Pour votre chaise de pont, voyez le steward du pont. Votre garçon de cabine verra à la préparation de votre bain, à l'heure qui vous conviendra	voo pooreh rert'neer votr' plahssˆah tahbl' ahn voozˆadraissahn oh maitr' dohtel dahn lah sahl ah mahnzheh. poor votr shaiz der pon, vwahyeh ler steward deū pon. votr gahrson der kabeen vairrah ah lah prehparahs'yon der votr ban, ah lēr kee voo conv'yandrah

Steward

At what hour would you like to take your bath?	A quelle heure aimeriez-vous prendre votre bain?	ah kellˆēr aim'r'yeh-voo prahndr' votr' ban
I will see to it that your dinner clothes are ready for you to dress for dinner	Je verrai à ce que votre "smoking" soit prêt avant dîner	zher vairreh ahss ker votr' smoking swah prai ahvahn deeneh

Italic r and i silent; thick n indicates nasal; apostrophe indicates suppressed vowel.

English	French	Pronunciation
If you wish, I will clean and press your clothes	*Si vous le désirez, je ferai nettoyer et presser vos vêterments*	see voo ler dehzeereh, zher f'reh nettwahyeh ai praisseh voh vait'-mah**n**
Your shoes will be cleaned if you will leave them at the door of your room	*Vos chaussures seront cirées si vous les déposez à la porte de votre chambre*	voh shohsseûr s'ro**n** seereh see voo lai dehpohzeh ah la pohrt de**r** votr shah**n**br'
I have been told to give you this package.	*On m'a prié de vous remettre ce paquet*	o**n** mah preeyeh de**r** voo rermai'tr' se**r** pahkai
Will you have your trunks ready so that I may take them at the appointed time?	*Veuillez préparer vos malles afin qu'on puisse les prendre à l'heure fixée*	vēryeh prehpahreh voh mahl ahfa**n** ko**n** peûeess lai prah**n**dr' ah lēr feexeh
I trust that you have enjoyed the voyage, and that we will again have the pleasure of numbering you among our passengers	*J'espère que vous avez aimé la traversée et que nous aurons encore le plaisir de vous compter au nombre de nos passagers*	zhaispair ke**r** vooz^ahvehz^aimeh lah trahvairsseh ai ke**r** nooz^ohro**n**z^ahkohr le**r** plaizeer de**r** voo conteh oh no**n**br' de**r** noh passahzheh

Purser

Here is a letter for you	*Voici une lettre pour vous*	vwahsee eûn lettr poor voo
How much do you desire in banknotes and in change?	*Combien désirez-vous en billets de banque et en monnaie?*	konb'ya**n** dehzeereh-voo ah**n** bee'yai de**r** bah**n**k ai ah**n** munnai?
The cost of a radiotelephone message to . . . is $ . . .	*Le coût d'un message radiophonique à . . est de $ . . .*	ler koo du**n** messahzh rahdeeohfohneek ah . . . ai de**r** $ . . .

Italic *r* and *i* silent; thick **n** indicates nasal; apostrophe indicates suppressed vowel.

INDEX

	PAGE
Accent, Tonic	9
Accents	14
Accessories of Bicycle	50
Accessories of Motor	52
Accommodation (Hotel)	114-117
Addressing Persons, Note on	95
Adjectives (Alphabetical list of)	76
Adjectives (Tables of)	91
Adverbs	86
Afternoon Tea	117
Agricultural Terms	24
Ailments	32
Airmail	118
Alphabet, The	9
American Money	120
Amusements	48, 126
Animals	20
Articles, The	8
Auxiliary Verbs	93, 94
Avoir (to have)	93
Baggage	107, 113, 125, 155
Barbershop	115
Baths	115, 156
Bedroom	128
Beverages	34, 121, 122
Bicycle	50
Bill (Hotel), The	117, 120
Birds	20
Bodily Powers	31
Body, The	30
Booking (by Rail)	104-114
Booking (by Steamship)	153
Book-keeping	59
Boots and Shoes	37
Breakfast	34, 121, 123
Buildings (Public)	24, 123
Bus	44
Business	59
Cab	44, 123
Cabin	154
Car	124
Check (baggage)	107
Cigarettes	126
Coaching	44
Colloquial Expressions	97
Colours	24
Commercial Terms	59
Concert	48
Conjunctions	86

	PAGE
Consonants, Combinations of	14
Cooking	34, 36
Correspondence	57
Countries, Names of	42
Country, The	24
Cries (of Animals)	20
Customs, The	113, 139, 140
Cycling	50
Dancing	117
Days of the Week	27
Declaration (Customs)	113
Dimensions	31
Dinner	34, 121
Diphthongs	13
Diseases	32
Doctor	33
Dog	112
Dress	37
Dress Materials	37
Drink (Beverages)	34, 121, 122
Drug Store	125
Emotion, Expressions of	101
Emotions, The	31
English Money	151
Enquiries	102
Etre (to be)	94
Exchange in Small Sums	150
Express	137-153
Finance	59
Fishes	20
Flowers	22
Food	34
French Equivalents (of English phrases)	9
Fruits	22
Furniture	40
Games	48
Garage	124
Gender	8
Greetings	95, 134
Health	32
Hockey	131
Holidays	28
Hotel	114-128
House	40
Human Body	30

	PAGE
Ice Water	125
Insects	22
Insurance	62
Introductory Remarks	7
Judicial Terms	64
Land (Physical Features)	18
Laundry	125, 126, 127
Legal Terms	64
Luggage (See Baggage)	45
Mails	118, 119, 126
Mankind	29
Medical Terms	32
Mental Powers	31
Messages to Ships	136, 137
Messengers	131, 133
Metals	19
Method of Study	16
Military Terms	68
Military Titles	67
Minerals	19
Missionaries, Terms for	71
Money, Changing	117, 157
Money Order, and etc.	56, 149, 150
Months	27
Modes of Address	95
Motoring	52, 124
Nasal Sound	15
Nature	17
Naval Terms	68
Naval Titles	67
Night Clubs	126
Numbers, Cardinal	74
" Collective	75
" Distributive	75
" Ordinal	75
Occupations	58
Officials, Ranks and Titles of	67
Parcels	147
Passport	114, 154
Pastimes	48
Personal Identification	129
Phonetic System	7
Photography	54
Physical Qualities	31
Polite Expressions	95
Post	56, 126
Precious Stones	19
Prepositions	86
Professions	58
Pronouns, Tables of	91, 92
Pronunciation	8

	PAGE
Railway	44, 104-114
Ranks, (Official, and etc.)	67
Registering (luggage)	107
Relations (relatives)	29
Religion	71
Remedies (Medical and etc.)	32, 125
Reptiles	22
Rooms	40, 124
Sample Tables	116
Seasons	28
Senses, The	32
Shipments by Express	137-148
Shipping	46
Shoemaker	125
Sleeping Car	108, 109, 111, 113
Smoking	36
Speed, Motoring	53
Steamship Travel	46, 47, 153-157
Stewards	156
Store (Departmental)	124
Table Utensils	36
Taxi	123
Tea	117
Telegraph	56, 117, 119, 128-137
Telephone	57, 120, 133, 136
Theatre	49, 126
Tickets	45, 104-113, 155
Titles	67
Toilet Requisites	37
Town, In	123
Towns	43
Trades	58
Trading	59
Train	44, 105-114
Tram	45
Travellers' Cheques	112, 120, 150-153
Travelling by Rail	44, 104-114
Travelling by Sea	46, 153-157
Trees	22
Typewriting	57
Utensils, Cooking and Table	36
Valet Service	125, 157
Vegetables	22
Verbs, Auxiliary	93
Vowel Combinations	12
Washing List	39
Water (Natural Divisions)	18
Weather	116, 131
World (Natural Phenomena)	17
Writing Paper	127

BOOKS RECOMMENDED FOR
FURTHER READING

HUGO'S FRENCH SIMPLIFIED.   The Hugo Simplified System.
> TORONTO: THE MUSSON BOOK COMPANY LTD.   Cloth $1.50

MUSSON'S IMPROVED DICTIONARY OF THE FRENCH AND
ENGLISH LANGUAGES.   By J. O. Kettridge, with phonetic
transcription of every French vocabulary word.   526 pages.
> TORONTO: THE MUSSON BOOK COMPANY LTD.   Cloth $1.25

E.F.G. POCKET PRONOUNCING FRENCH-ENGLISH, ENGLISH-
FRENCH DICTIONARY.   By A. Mendel,   628 pages.
> TORONTO: THE MUSSON BOOK COMPANY LTD.   Cloth $0.60
> Leather $1.00

L'ANGLAIS SANS MAITRE (ENGLISH SELF-TAUGHT FOR THE
FRENCH).   By the natural method with phonetic pronunciation.
Thimm's System.
> TORONTO: THE MUSSON BOOK COMPANY LTD.   Limp cloth $0.60

WESSELY'S IMPROVED FRENCH-ENGLISH, ENGLISH-FRENCH
DICTIONARY.   By J. E. Wessely, improved and enlarged by
Latham and Curle.   628 pages.
> TORONTO: THE MUSSON BOOK COMPANY LTD.
> School Edition, Cloth $0.60

BRUSH UP YOUR FRENCH (First and Second Series).
> TORONTO: J. M. DENT & SONS.

BRUSH UP YOUR FRENCH (Commercial Series).
> TORONTO: J. M. DENT & SONS.

FRENCH COMMERCIAL TERMS AND PHRASES. Prof. R. Lusum.
> TORONTO: J. M. DENT & SONS. $1.00

NELSON'S FIRST FRENCH COURSE (An Introduction to Spoken
French).   R. L. Graeme Ritchie and James M. Moore.
> TORONTO: THOMAS NELSON & SONS. $0.60

APPRENONS LE FRANCAIS.   Edith L. Atkin.
> TORONTO: SIR ISAAC PITMAN & SONS.

PREMIER COURS DE FRANCAIS.   Louis A. Roux.
> TORONTO: THE MACMILLAN COMPANY OF CANADA LIMITED.

BASIC FRENCH.   Cochran-Eddy Redfield.
> D. C. HEATH & COMPANY.
> TORONTO: THE COPP-CLARK COMPANY LTD.